Quote

Yesterday is history.
Tomorrow is a mystery.
And today is a gift.
That's why it is called, the present.

Alice Morse Earle

Dedication

Bat Tales is dedicated to three people who have passed away: my father George Batmale (Pops), lifelong best friend David Johnson (DJ), and writing mentor Karen Chamberlain.

Pops and DJ had an easygoing nature. They laughed often and loved having a good time. DJ was extremely adventurous. Both were men of few words, and each possessed a stellar dry sense of humor and a brilliant mind. The value of being blessed with a wonderful father and fifty-year best friend cannot be put into words. I will be grateful to them forever.

Karen Chamberlain co-founded the Aspen Writer's Foundation and later the Glenwood Springs Writer's Workshop. She was a gifted and acclaimed poet and author. Karen embraced and skillfully guided every writer— regardless of ability or age. Heart mattered most to Karen.

Bat Tales is also dedicated to two groups of people. First, the current and former members of the Glenwood Springs Writers' Workshop (GSWW). Second, the people who struggle with reading. I had a difficult time learning to read. But when I was nine or ten-years-old—during summer and under no classroom pressure—I discovered the joy of reading books. My hope is that someone might find this book and it will spark a love of written words.

Without the members of the GSWW this book *abso-*

Bat Tales

Bat Tales

True Stories of Adventure, Nature, Wildlife and Life

C.C. & a lover of skiing, hiking and the outdoors. Hope you enjoy my work.

Mark "Batman"

Mark Batmale
"Batman"

Cisco Publishing

Cisco Publishing
P.O. Box 2107, Basalt, Colorado 81621
Printed in the United States of America

Cisco Publishing

FIRST EDITION

Written by Mark Batmale
Photographs Copyright © Mark Batmale
unless otherwise mentioned.
Book design and cover, co-designed
by Mark Batmale and Cindy Rogers.
Ms. Rogers' websites:
treedogpress.com
collectionsfromanaspenchef.com

ISBN Hardcover 978-0-9975997-0-1
ISBN Paperback 978-0-9975997-1-8
ISBN eBook 978-0-9975997-2-5

Website: battales.net

lutely would not have been possible. Their keen insight and constructive comments were always respectfully given, and quite often with a great deal of humor. When I first attended the group I felt like a third grader with the college kids—but was lovingly accepted.

The dedication is longer than normal because this is my first book, and life is uncertain. It is important to me that I honor the people mentioned and this may be my one opportunity.

Contents

Author's Note

Bat Tales is a work of nonfiction. The stories have been presented to the best of my memory. I have tried to take very little literary license. The dialogue, however, is not exact; it's impossible to remember precisely how someone said something decades ago. Dialogue has also been added in places to facilitate sharing the stories.

Numerous people allowed me to use their real names. And when it was impossible to reconnect with someone, occasionally, I made the assumption that it would be okay to use their given name. However, for various reasons, some names have been changed.

Batmale is French. My paternal grandparents are from the Pyrenees Mountains in southern France, near the city of Pau. The name is unique. I've never met, or heard of anyone, with the name Batmale who is not a relative.

My last name has been mispronounced all my life; I've gotten used to it. Most of my friends who have a difficult last name to pronounce know how to correctly say Batmale, there's a kinship. Here's an easy way to pronounce the funny French name. (I mention this only because some readers might be curious.) Look at the sentence: We wanted a *bottle* of beer after the bear almost *mauled* us. Take the BOT from bottle and add it to MAUL. Voila, Batmale is pronounced Bot-maul.

Nicknames pick us, we don't choose them. And those

who receive a nickname have a variety of feelings about the name bestowed or forced upon them, which range from love to loathing. About the nickname Batman—it's a long story. But briefly, the change from Batmale to Batman is easy to see. When I was young, I strongly disliked being called Batman. I thought the 1960s television show, *Batman*, was a bit dumb, bat-mobile, bat-cave, holy-bat-crap... Plus I was the smallest kid in my class; I was no superhero. But after half a century and a better sense of humor, I've finally warmed to the nickname. So I guess by using "Batman" on the cover of this book, I'm fully embracing the name that picked me. In addition, my parents didn't give me a middle name; they thought Batmale was enough of a mouthful.

My apologies for going on and on about the name stuff, but I wanted to answer the questions that other writers like Smith, Miller, Johnson... never need to explain.

All the photographs are by the author unless noted.

At the end of several stories, there are a few paragraphs which I have called "Extra Bits." I believe that in any story, or life, there is always more that can be said. When I was writing some of the stories there was often a little bit more I wanted to include. But those pieces didn't quite fit in or mesh with the story, they felt awkwardly inserted or tacked on. I decided to include the extra pieces after the end of the story. I debated what to call them, afterword, anecdote, or epilogue. Extra bits came to mind, the term matches my informal attitude.

To the reader: Thank you for holding this book or device in your hands and reading my work. I sincerely hope you enjoy these words.

Lost Mates

Eagles on the Highway

Mount Wayah

Eagles on the Highway

"Eagles On Highway" and "No Services Next 107 Miles" are two of my favorite road signs. The unusual signs are on Interstate 70 in eastern Utah, twenty-five miles apart. Is there a correlation or connection between the two signs other than long lines of yellow and white paint, or miles of asphalt complete with rumble strips? I believe eagles make their home in the area because of the lack of human activity. Some creatures need a "non-serviced" environment to survive and thrive.

And why are eagles on the highway? My guess is they are on the road because of an abundance of road-killed rabbits and other unfortunate critters, resulting in easy dining.

I was driving to a familiar patch of desert, a quiet place, somewhere in the middle of nowhere, with a plan to camp for a few days. Along the way, near my campsite, I spotted two golden eagles. They were perched together, wing to wing, on the rim of a small unnamed canyon. A few friends and I call the nameless canyon "Sage Canyon." The pair was near Interstate 70, in the vicinity of the two signs.

Thrilled by the sight of not one but two goldens, I stopped and watched the majestic birds for a minute or two. I was parked a little over a hundred yards from the eagles, and I wanted to rummage around the backseat and find my binoculars and get a closer look. The keen-eyed couple, with their superior vision, already had their "binoculars" focused on me.

I didn't reach for the binoculars. I sensed that if I made too much movement or stayed too long they would fly away. It was not my style to disturb or bother the native couple and I was invading their space. Rather than catching a glimpse, I could have gawked at the pair for a long time. This was not an everyday event. But it felt best to briefly enjoy the moment and move on. Better to leave, than overstay my unwelcome.

After a few days of camping it was time to head home. On my way there I looked for the eagles when I drove up and out of Sage Canyon, but the goldens were nowhere to be seen. I parked at the top of the canyon, and decided to walk along the rim and go to the spot where the pair had been resting. Maybe I would find an eagle feather? I knew there was not much chance. The weather had been very windy, typical for springtime in the Utah desert. Like the red sand of Utah, which occasionally gets blown to the mountains of Colorado and subtly pinkens the white snow, an eagle feather would have blown far from the rim.

I found the exact place where the two had perched, confirmed by an eagle-sized, freshly dried puddle of white chalky pee. For an unknown reason I touched the white spot, perhaps to complete the experience.

My good friend Tom is a gnarly, rusty and crusty old rock climber, with notable first ascents he never talks about. He is an extremely observant character, often limping and always with a set of binoculars around his neck. His strained walk is caused by a gimpy ankle, which is part of the price Tom paid for his time on the rock. We treasure and share the same quiet patch of desert, sometimes together, but most often on our own.

What we don't share are walking styles and observational skills. I stride along sunny ridge tops, eyes gazing at the distant horizon, enjoying the view. My head is sometimes in the clouds. I am most often an observer of only the obvious. Tom kicks rocks and finds fossils. He scuffs around in the shade at the base of cliff faces, intently looking for whatever might appear. Well off the beaten path, he has found one hundred year old inscriptions and artwork carved by generations of shepherds. And he's spied many elusive critters, both in the air and on the ground. Tom's limp and slow gait have magnified his powers of observation.

One night Tom and I were camped together in the desert. It was about two years before I'd seen the pair of eagles on the rim of Sage Canyon. I knew Tom's ankle was hurting. Hoping to ease or somewhat "justify" the pain, I said, "Tom, the slower one goes the more one sees." He didn't appreciate my trite but true statement and only grunted—or was it a low growl?

Later that night Tom opened up and started talking. He said, "A couple months ago I found half an eagle carcass. The carcass was under the power line near Sage Canyon." Guilty of no crime, except having a massive wingspan, the innocent bird appeared to have been electrocuted. It was killed because its wings accidentally bridged two powerfully charged wires.

$\sim$

Three weeks after I spotted the two eagles at Sage Canyon, I was alone and heading back to my old familiar patch of desert. I looked for the goldens when I drove past their place on the rim of Sage Canyon, but the pair wasn't there. While in camp, I remembered Tom's story about finding the carcass of an electrocuted eagle. The next morning I decided to walk under the power line and look for the remains of Tom's eagle. My goals were simple, walk somewhere new, enjoy the sunny and windless day, and perhaps find an eagle feather.

I drove close to the power line and parked. The dirt road dead-ended at a high point near the electrified line. Two hundred feet from the tallest power pole, I shouldered my daypack and started walking. But I only went a few steps, when I saw something that stopped me cold. Lying on the ground at the base of the tallest power pole, together and touching, were two golden eagles. The pair looked perfect—except they were dead.

Solemnly, I walked closer and closer. No binoculars were needed. I was not bothering or disturbing them. I was the one disturbed and heartbroken. The electrocuted mates were huge. Were they the same pair I'd seen perched on the rim of Sage Canyon only three weeks earlier? They had to be. Sage Canyon and the power pole were only a mile and a half apart. As fate would have it, one's head was peacefully nestled in the others chest. And their golden, yellow-brown eyes, which had once watched me, were wide open. They might have mated for life and now ...

Did I want to cry? Yes.

Was I crying? Only inside.

The situation was so final. What could I do, if anything? I wanted to give them a more fitting resting place by burying them together. I love the desert animals and know they need to eat, but I didn't want this pair to become carrion and torn to pieces.

Even touching the pair might be unlawful. Burying them was seriously illegal, but in my mind it would have been okay. I didn't have a shovel and the idea was overwhelming, especially being alone. If Tom and I had been together, after being stunned speechless, I probably would have asked him, "Should we bury them?"

In his quirky way, Tom might have tried to soften and ease the moment by saying, "They're just big brown birds. We should pluck'em and cook'em." Followed by, "Who cares about the Feds, let's get the shovels."

Utterly dejected, forty-five minutes after finding the goldens, I simply drove away. But before I left the tragic pair, I needed to do one thing. Uncomfortable and ill at ease, I knelt down next to the big-eyed birds of prey. With great reverence and respect, I gently brushed my hand across each of the incredible beings.

As I drove away, on what truly felt like a dead-end road, I saw a truck approaching in the distance. I pulled over, rolled down my window, and waited for the truck to arrive. I was not in the mood for talking, but in the mood for *life* and human contact. I also wanted to find out if the driver knew about the eagles. The pickup truck slowed but didn't stop.

The driver, stern and stone-faced, kept his eyes forward. He never glanced in my direction. No eye to eye contact. Not even one finger limply lifted off the steering wheel for a weak wave. People *always* stopped, or at least waved, in that remote area. When the white truck passed I saw a government emblem on the door, though I couldn't discern which division. My guess is that the employee knew what was at the end of the road. He was on a sad and depressing mission; he wasn't in the mood to talk either.

I moved on and parked a little over a mile from the birds. Then I grabbed my binoculars and could see that the official vehicle had stopped at the murderous power pole. Twenty minutes passed and the government truck remained parked. Looking through the binoculars, I could determine nothing and moved on. Several hours later, at dusk, I returned to the pole to satisfy my curiosity. The majestic pair was gone.

∼

Months later, I drove up the dead-end road and returned to the scene. Just because... To my amazement, I found a line of power poles unlike any I had ever seen. The offending pole and twenty-five adjacent poles had been changed. The old **T**-shaped power poles (pole with a crossbar on top) had been modified to **I**-shaped power poles (pole only). And the two electrical lines had been repositioned; they were no longer mounted to the crossbar, at equal heights, level and parallel to each other. Both electrical wires were now mounted to the **I**-shaped pole, with one wire above the other.

Was I relieved to think it should never happen again? Yes. Yet the image of the golden pair remains vivid and haunting.

The Utah Department of Transportation has rechecked the mileage on I-70 and changed many signs. The former sign said 107 miles.

New **I**-shaped pole.

Old **T**-shaped pole, which has been modified to include a bird perch. Golden eagle on perch.

Mount Wayah

Early one Fourth of July morning, Katie and I drove to an out-of-the-way trailhead. We parked at a lofty 10,000 feet, near the Continental Divide in the Colorado Rockies, on a glorious Independence Day. The parking lot was empty. To our surprise we saw a lone backpacker sitting under a spruce tree.

We waved to each other, and the backpacker rose and walked towards us. The hiker introduced himself; his name was Chris. He asked us, "I've been backpacking for a few weeks. Would you mind taking out a small bag of trash?" Katie and I were happy to help. Chris handed me the heaviest and most densely packed small Ziploc baggie I had ever held.

"Where are you headed?" I asked.

"Oregon."

I remember thinking to myself, *Wow, this guy is walking from Colorado to Oregon.*

Knowing fresh food is always a special treat on a long backpacking trip, I offered Chris an apple and one of my two freshly baked items. I let him choose which of the baked goods he wanted and our conversation started to flow. I mentioned to Chris, "The mountains in Colorado are incredible during July. But the next state on your way is Utah and it's stifling hot in July."

"I have water cached in many places and plan to hike

during the coolest part of the day—nighttime." Chris replied.

I began to think, *this guy is not a typical long distance backpacker*. My thought was quickly confirmed, when Chris casually told us, "This is my seventeenth, one-thousand-mile walk." Now I was more than wowed. I had never met anyone like him.

As we talked, Katie and I began to learn about Chris' journeys. He has been walking unique long lines in the wilderness and climbing peaks all along his routes. His one-thousand-mile treks have been much different than stepping onto the Pacific Crest, Appalachian, or Continental Divide Trails and marching miles. I believe Chris has walked some miles on those well-established trails, but maybe not. The Appalachian Trail runs from Georgia to Maine, and the Pacific Crest and Continental trails go from Mexico to Canada, border to border. All three of the trekking "highways" run north and south— Chris is walking east to west.

17,000 miles... Millions and millions of steps... I wish I knew more about Chris' journeys. Think about walking one thousand miles. Now ponder *seventeen*, one-thousand-mile walks.

Sadly, this was Chris' first trip without his four-legged partner, Wayah. Wayah was an Alaskan malamute, a dog who looked like a wolf. The word "wayah" is Cherokee for wolf. Scientists believe all dogs have descended from wolves. And Wayah, with his name, appearance, and lifestyle (spending most of his time in the mountains) seemed like a true descendant.

When Wayah's health completely failed, Chris suffered grief in the magnitude of losing a child. With no choice, Chris had Wayah "put down" and laid to rest. I have heard it said that the saddest thing about special dogs is that they do not live long enough. Chris understood this all too well. From our conversation with him, it was clear that the loneliness of his first trip without his four-legged brother was brutal.

While we talked, Katie told Chris about a malamute that she once had. Katie's dog was named Wolf. This struck the three of us as a remarkable coincidence. Wolf had been shot dead in the prime of his life, because he was mistaken for a wolf. He was killed in the mountains of Wyoming by a truly mistaken and misguided man. Not everyone loves or even tolerates wolves. Sharing stories and feelings about Wolf and Wayah had our hearts connecting.

The next two-and-a-half hours flashed by in conversation. The three of us talked about peaks and mountain ranges, the desert, and a very remote place in Wyoming called The Thoroughfare. We chatted about animals, big cats (mountain lions), bear scares and a goofy moose. Chris carried a radio and listened to music and NPR (National Public Radio). It was a presidential election year and *he* brought up politics. We talked a little about our political heroes and those we liked less. Chris, Katie and I shared a mutual love of wilderness, and discussed its unique and irreplaceable value. We also touched on a wide variety of topics: working and not working, shoes and socks, climbing mountains, traveling on foot-paths versus the expressway, weather both vicious and blissful, and the joy of sleeping under the stars.

I wanted to turn Chris' pack upside down to see everything that a person who has walked a distance of more than halfway around the world was carrying. What was he eating? What clothing did he have, besides the long-sleeved tee-shirt, dark nylon shorts, and ankle high gaiters that he wore? What did he sleep in, on, and under? In addition to his radio, did he carry any other luxuries? Did he keep a journal? Without asking, I was certain he did.

During our time together, Chris told us about his hike the previous day, July third. Chris had climbed an unnamed, 13,000-foot mountain. He had christened the anonymous peak and gave it a wonderful name, Mount Wayah. On the summit he placed a small waterproof tube. The tube contained a sign-in register and a simple shrine dedicated to his dog Wayah. In the tube, Chris had placed a photo of Wayah and one handwritten page expressing his respect and love.

We could have visited all day, but finally Chris said, "You two need to go hiking." We hugged, shook hands, said good-bye, and hugged again. Many weeks later I received a letter from Chris with an Oregon postmark. I was thrilled and quickly wrote back. To my great disappointment, the letter I wrote to Chris reappeared in my mailbox; it was marked by the post office "No Such Address."

In the past eleven years I have hiked to the summit of Mt. Wayah three times. Each time I left a new note for Chris in the small tube on top of the peak hoping to reconnect with him. I am still overflowing with curiosity about Chris and Wayah. Our visit on the Fourth of July was not enough time together. So many questions remain about this new friend. I know some year Chris will return to Mt. Wayah to honor his beloved dog, and hopefully see my note.

On my first hike up Mount Wayah I sat on the summit and copied, word for word, Chris' page of dedication and love.

This register has been placed here in memory of Wayah the Malamute. The best partner a long distance backpacker could hope for. In only seven far too short years he led the way across 14,000 miles in twelve trips. Well over half his life was spent in the wilderness of the Rocky Mtns. Born in Colorado, raised in the Rockies, he did it all...swam raging rivers, crossed the desert, climbed glaciers and snowfields, growled at a Grizzly bear and ducked a charging bull moose. He climbed 157 peaks. He loved the wilderness like no other dog I've ever seen. I'll never forget the joy and companionship he brought to me on our trips. I can't tell you how different the wilderness is without you. Wayah, I'll always remember.

Love, Chris

"I never met a man I liked better than my dog"—The Rank Rodent (Chris' nickname)

Wayah the Malamute
Born: May 10, 1993, Longmont, Colorado.
Passed: August 2, 2000, Hamilton, Montana.

Note to Chris:

Dear Chris

I hope you don't mind this story being printed.
I also hope the story brings us together again.

Your friend, Mark

Waterproof tube and sign-in register on the top of
Mount Wayah.

Whimsy

Dumb, Dumber and Dumbest

The Perfect Tool

Dumb, Dumber and Dumbest

A trio of outdoorsy twenty-one year-olds, from suburban Northern California, was adventuring in British Columbia and Alberta, Canada. When the three returned from a hike at Pyramid Lake, near the town of Jasper, they found a bear next to their Buick. The black bear was drinking from a carton of chocolate milk, which Dumb had dumbly left outside their Skylark convertible. Dumbest said with confidence, "If we make a bunch of noise we can shoo it away."

In the past, each of the three had encountered "pesky" bears in Yosemite National Park in California. Yosemite is famous for granite and notorious for "problem" bears. At Yosemite, they had watched sensible adults bang pots and pans together to successfully remove bears from campsites. Dumbest had done so himself.

Dumbest was confident all the time, unlike the shy and insecure duo of Dumb and Dumber. Dumbest had all the answers—all the time. He could be a bit much. Dumbest led the way clapping hands and yelling, "Go find some honey. Go back to your honey. Shoo!"

Unfazed, the bruin kept right on slurping. Using a shred of common sense, the guys stopped short of the bear. The three backed away and huddled. "Do we need more noise? Yeah, more noise." Dumbest added, "I wish I could get our pots and pans." But his favorite noise-making tools were in the Buick's trunk.

Once again the team walked forward yelling. Their second attempt was also unsuccessful. But after they retreated, the bruin hopped onto the trunk of the Buick and stared at the three. Or, was the bruin annoyed and glaring?

There were a few important facts the young trio had not learned about bears, and life. First, were some of the things to do and *not do* when encountering a bear. Another thing was a little bit about bear behavior, and that direct eye-to-eye contact with a bear is not a good thing. This pertains to dominance and submission. If a bashful bear is staring at you, you might have a big problem. The most important fact—yet to be fully learned by the three—was that material things are worth nothing compared to people's lives, health, and safety.

Dumbest was worried about the white canvas top on the convertible. It was his first car. A third attempt to shoo the bruin worked and the upset bear did get off the car. But unfortunately, the bear's reason for doing so was to follow the three as they retreated. They were walking away and the bear was walking twenty-five yards behind. No one with two legs, or four legs, was running or swimming—yet.

Where to go? Pyramid Lake encircled a tiny island with a connecting foot-bridge. The narrow bridge was forty yards long and just wide enough for single-file travel, with no room to pass. The island had two buildings, a small rain shelter near the water's edge and an outhouse. The rain shelter didn't have walls, and its simple hip roof was supported by twelve posts, each the diameter of a telephone pole. The outhouse was small, but at least it had a door to hide behind.

Dumb, Dumber and Dumbest headed across the bridge, like the calamity prone and dopey Three Stooges, Moe,

Larry and Curly. Dumb was first on the bridge, next came Dumbest, then Dumber, and last in line—The Bear. Dumb stopped for a second to glance over his shoulder, and his pause caused a domino-like chain reaction. The desperate dorks resembled the Stooges as they stumbled and bumbled into each other.

Dumbest yelled. "I'm going to the outhouse!" It was an appropriate place, because the guys were scared and the outhouse was the perfect spot for an "accident". Dumb and Dumber hustled in a different direction, to the rain shelter.

The smartest move of the day was made by Dumb. When he first set foot on the island, without slowing down, he dropped-and-ditched his day-pack which contained left-overs from lunch. The bear and his nose switched focus and stopped at the pack. Then the bruin shredded the pack and finished Dumb's lunch.

At the base of the rain shelter, Dumb interlocked his fingers and cupped his hands. No words were exchanged as Dumber stepped into the cupped hands. Dumb lifted and pushed, and Dumber worked his way onto the roof. Once "safely" on the roof, Dumber reached over the edge and dangled his arm like a rope. Dumb, light and lanky, climbed Dumber's arm as Dumber pulled him onto the roof.

At first glance the outhouse looked stout, but it was built like a flimsy plastic porta-potty. Dumbest quickly decided the outhouse was a poor choice and hurried to the rain shelter. Standing on the ground alone and forlorn, the look on Dumbest's face mirrored what each of the three were feeling—terror. Dumb and Dumber, the insecure twosome, looked at each other for a split-second. They didn't smile, but when their eyes met they twinkled, because this time they had *all* the answers. And the two of them were the *only* solution for Dumbest's big, big problem. Quickly, without a word spoken, they hoisted their friend.

A bit relieved, the three moved away from the edge and up the low angled roof to the ridge. A minute or two later, not three or four, the bear arrived. The bruin circled the rain shelter glancing up at trio, obviously ticked off with them. Then the bear disappeared beneath the roof of the building. An instant later the rain shelter shook and vibrated like a subtle earthquake, yet different from any the Californians had ever felt.

Dumb, Dumber and Dumbest looked at each other with alarmed and despondent eyes. No one said a word. Was the bear trying to climb the building? Black bears are excellent climbers.

Imagine—a black furry arm, thick and strong, with a paw that includes long knife-like claws. It appears from below and reaches toward you. You fully understand its intention, and not one word of pleading will help.

Fight or flight? If the bear reached the roof it would be mayhem, a free-for-all, every dummy for himself. The three would have scattered, and been running or swimming for their lives. The classic bear tale would become reality: *You don't have to run faster than a bear. You just have to run faster than your friend.*

Fortunately the rain shelter had been constructed with a long eave. The distance from the top of a post to the roof was a lengthy reach. When the bruin came out from under the building it batted and pounded on a nearby trash can, like it was a cheap thin aluminum can. A minute later, for some unknown reason, the bear lost interest, crossed the bridge and scampered away. Dumbest and Dumber had seen the bear start over the bridge and leave; they jumped down. Dumb remained glued to the roof until he was convinced it was safe.

The three then drove away to camp for the evening, with no destination in mind. But anywhere would be better than Pyramid Lake. For the first and only time, the three-pack spent the night together in the Buick. Dumbest told Dumb, "You saved our butts today by dropping your pack. You should take the back seat. Dumber and I can sleep in front."

Safely tucked into the Skylark, they talked before falling asleep. Dumbest made a bold statement, "If I saw the bear's paw reach over the edge of the roof, I was ready to smash and kick it with my waffle stompers (heavy leather hiking boots)."

Dumb told him, "Dumbest, we know you would have. We're just glad you didn't have to try." Dumb was an excellent swimmer and added, "If I saw a paw and then the bear, I would have jumped in the lake and been swimming for it."

Before drifting off to sleep, in silence and alone with their own thoughts, each knew they had been lucky. And they were grateful the lessons learned had been pain-free. The trio of friends, in addition to sharing the Buick for the night, now shared a new name—Wiser.

～

The author is one of the three characters. In truth, no one was dumb, dumber, or dumbest. The three of us equally shared in our "dummyness." I labeled us dummies because at no point did one of us step up and say: "Quit shooing the bear." or "This is stupid." or "Stop!"

We each have different recollections of the incident—mostly about what the bear did when it got to the rain shelter. Because we were on the roof, none of us could see exactly what the bear did. Two of us remember the building shaking. Thirty-plus years have passed and we have remained friends.

Extra Bits

Every living creature is mindful of their next meal, including bears, and they have big, big appetites. The bad rub between bruins and humans begins when bears discover and acquire a taste for easily available human food and garbage. The bumper sticker "A Fed Bear Is A Dead Bear" is sadly sometimes true.

Dumb and Dumber moved to a Colorado ski resort four weeks after their bear scare. Their plan was to stay for one ski season. Dumber stayed in Colorado eight weeks. Dumb has called Colorado home for almost forty years.

During Dumb's first twenty-five years in Colorado he saw only one bear. But in the last decade, bear sightings and encounters have increased exponentially where he lives. Drought is part of the problem, because without water the bruin's natural food sources have not grown. A few years ago, Dumb awoke to find three small, cuddly bear cubs playfully batting and biting a rope swing in his yard. Big Mama sat ten feet from the front door and watched her youngsters play. Mom was huge.

Later that summer, Dumb was hiking behind his home along an overgrown irrigation ditch. Unintentionally, he was making a lot of noise by stepping on dried branches and also breaking the overgrown vegetation with his hands and arms. Dumb barely heard a low growl. Then he clearly heard the sound a second time and stopped. He looked up to see a bear only yards away. But unlike at Pyramid Lake, this time the bear was the scared one and it was climbing a tree to escape.

Sadly, during one recent summer, twenty-seven "problem" bears were destroyed in and near the town where Dumb lives. According to a newspaper article in the *Aspen Daily News*: "Wildlife officers so far this summer have had to euthanize 27 bears in the division's 4,800-square-mile region that encompasses Aspen, Glenwood Springs, Vail, and up to southern Routt County."

Dumber has a second home in the Sierra Nevada Mountains in California, which has been broken into and ransacked by a bear. He installed heavy wooden shutters to cover the windows and doors of his log cabin. The shutters now have claw marks.

Dumbest went on to an accomplished career in outdoor education. He retired early and became a sailing instructor. He now lives in a place where he's more likely to be attacked by a falling coconut than a bear.

Foot-bridge at Pyramid Lake.

Rain shelter with Pyramid Lake in background.

The Perfect Tool

Children are such children... Meaning kids are different than adults. They do, think, and say things only a kid can imagine.

When my seven-year-old stepdaughter, Ivy, asked if she could bring her pink butterfly net into the restaurant, my adult brain was thinking, *there are no butterflies to catch in a restaurant.* I could understand a coloring book and crayons, or a stuffed animal to talk with, perhaps a book to read, or some toy she could play with at the table— but a butterfly net? I didn't ask her why, I just said, "Yeah sure." So when Ivy walked into the restaurant carrying her pink net I didn't think much of it. It's a kid thing.

Sometimes, doesn't it feel as if everything seems to happen all at once? Partway through dinner, Ivy and her mom, Annie, needed to visit the restroom. Only a minute later, a small bird flew inside the restaurant, and it slammed hard and loud into a large corner window. Six very shocked diners seated next to the window shrieked and screamed. Panicked, the bird flapped wildly and moved all around the window trying to escape. The frantic restaurant proprietor rushed over and hopelessly tried to gather the bird using his hands.

I couldn't believe the proprietor's good fortune as I hurried to his aid. Standing behind the restaurateur, I gently tapped his shoulder. And without saying a word or making eye contact, I simply reached around him and held the pink butterfly net in front of him. Miraculously, the perfect tool had appeared.

When Ivy and Annie returned from the restroom, I excitedly said, "Girls, you won't believe what just happened."

"We heard the screams and wondered what was going on." Annie replied.

As I recounted the story, Ivy gave me a doubting and dubious look. Without saying a word, I simply handed her the pink net which held five or six little feathers.

Pink butterfly net on the side of the author's garage.

Yikes!

"Check It Out!"

Close Calls in the Sandbox

"Check It Out!"

"Hike up the volcano. Then go to the edge and look into the crater," George strongly encouraged me. The two of us were acquaintances in the ski-town where we lived. By chance, we were sitting alone on a long slow ski lift with plenty of uninterrupted time.

While we moved up the mountain, I told George, "I'm leaving town for the winter. I'm going south." My non-itinerary had just one thing scheduled, a one-way flight to Mexico City—the very next day.

George shared with me that as a kid, he'd spent a few years in the small country of Guatemala, México's southern neighbor. His father was a diplomat. He also told me that a visit to a volcano, Volcan Pacaya, was the highlight of his years in Latin America. Volcan Pacaya had burned a lasting impression into his memory.

I had a tiny history with Guatemala as a kid. My brush with the country was a travel brochure I made while in middle school. I learned of the resplendent quetzal, considered by many bird lovers to be the most beautiful bird in the world. The quetzal is covered in brilliant red and green feathers, with a white chest and dashes of neon blue. Its plumage also includes streaming tail feathers over two feet long. The bird is so impressive and revered that the monetary unit in Guatemala is called the quetzal. An image of the bird adorns every paper bill and 25 *centavo* (cent) coin.

I also learned Guatemala is home to many Mayan ruins. Some remain hidden by overgrown jungle, but others have been discovered, uncovered, and rebuilt. Tikal is the most famous ruin, the exclamation point, and seven of its gigantic temples rise above the jungle canopy. The small nation is also home to distinctive and colorfully dressed native people, many of whom wear the traditional clothes of their village. They work the soil with simple hand tools and grow corn, beans, rice, coffee, and more corn, their staple. These indigenous people are the true native *Norte Americanos* (North Americans.) Their languages pre-date the invasion by the Spaniards, and for many of them Spanish is a second language.

The country has a mountainous region named The Highlands and a lowland rainforest known as the Petén. Inhabiting the tropical area are a variety of wildlife— parrots, toucans, monkeys, jaguars and deadly coral snakes. The vegetation varies from tiny delicate orange orchids to majestic Ceiba trees, Guatemala's national tree. Guatemala has one of the ten clearest lakes in the world, beautiful and spectacular Lago de Atitlan. At 1120 feet deep, the lake is the deepest in Central America; it's also endorheic, one that does not drain into the sea. On the Pacific coast are rare black sand beaches. The black sand is ground-up lava from active volcanoes.

George's words,*"Hike up the volcano. Then go to the edge, and look into the crater,"* had made an impression. Was an itinerary developing? No, but a seed that had been planted in school to visit Guatemala had been watered by my companion's words.

David, a London barrister, and I first met at a bus station in Oaxaca, Mexico. We were both traveling farther south. The two of us were moving from the city of Oaxaca, which is the capital city in the state of Oaxaca, and going to another capital city, San Cristobal de las Casas, in the state of Chiapas. Chiapas is the poorest and southernmost of México's thirty states. At that time, no incumbent Mexican president had *ever* visited the lowly state.

The bus was sold out, so David and I bought tickets for the following day. At David's suggestion, we got our assigned seats next to each other and in the first row, directly behind the driver. "Adios, see you tomorrow morning," he said, and we returned to our respective hotels.

The next morning we met back at the station and stepped onto the most posh bus I had ever seen. Lucky for us, because it was a *long* thirteen hour journey to San Cristobal de la Casas. The trip was filled with hours of animated conversation. Our bus ride started an adventuresome friendship, which lasted a brief but memorable fifteen days. Our paths would later diverge, only because David's time in Latin America and the United States was up; after traveling for six months he needed to get home to England.

Five days after our bus ride to San Cristobal de las Casas, David and I crossed the border into Guatemala. We had arrived at the *frontera* (border) in a very old and well-worn bus. The two of us were in Guatemala only a few days before we joined four other travelers and went to Antigua, Guatemala. We were in Antigua to watch an extravagant religious celebration on Good Friday, two days before Easter Sunday.

On the morning of Good Friday, we watched for hours as followers of the Catholic faith meticulously crafted colorful *alfombras* (carpets) on an asphalt street. The road was closed to traffic. The carpets were beautiful, intricate and large, twenty by fifty feet. Some were constructed with dyed sawdust, which was dampened to stay in place. Other carpets were made with flowers and petals. Very large stencils were used to make the designs for the *alfombras*.

While watching the carpets being constructed, I didn't realize that the street would be a parade route later that afternoon. The parade was a reenactment of Jesus' forced walk to his crucifixion. "Jesus" was dressed in a tattered loincloth and topped with a crown of thorns. His face and body were streaked with blood. I grew concerned when the people in the parade walked toward the *alfombras*. Then I was mildly horrified when they marched over and destroyed the beautiful short-lived artwork. (Many months later, back home, I picked up an issue of *National Geographic*. The magazine's cover was a photo taken at the elaborate parade in Antigua on Good Friday.)

Some travel is free flowing and fluid. During lunch on Good Friday, I talked with David and a few other travelers about Volcan Pacaya. Once in Guatemala I'd learned a little more about the volcano. By the end of lunch, we had a firm plan. On Easter Sunday, six of us would go to the small town of San Vincente de Pacaya and hike to the summit of Volcan Pacaya.

~

Volcan Pacaya has two summits and they are like fraternal twins. The only thing the two have in common is their height, which is about 8400 feet. One of the twins is a sleepy, quiet, inactive peak, where we planned to camp for the night. The second twin is a wide-awake, living and breathing, active volcano.

On Easter Sunday, while purchasing simple provisions and food from a small *tienda* (store), our group of six joined with another group of four travelers. Our six included three men (two British and one American) and three women (one German, one Canadian, and one American.) The other four were three German women and a Frenchman, Francois. As it turned out, the ten of us would be the only people on the mountain.

From the *tienda* we walked a short distance on a dirt road to the base of Volcan Pacaya. Hiking together, the group followed a simple footpath up the volcano. We trekked over and around different sized lava rocks and across fields of sandy ash. The mountain was burned and black and barren— it was completely devoid of vegetation. The volcano was nothing but rock, ash, and sand.

As we climbed the inactive twin we started to hear something. Every ten minutes or so, we heard what sounded like a distant jet engine; the sound lasted about thirty seconds. Did the volcano have a voice?

We reached the summit of the quiet twin a little before sunset. On top we found large blocks of lava, interspersed with nooks of sand. The black convoluted lava rocks were the size of dining tables that would seat six or eight. The patches of sand were a perfect place to sleep, and sleeping on this mountain would be unlike anyplace we had ever camped.

The sand was warm. Our soft sandy beds were heated— not by the sun— but by heat from within the Earth. I discovered this when I smoothed out the sand before laying out a tarp to sleep on. I told my companions, and we started digging our hands deep into the sand; the deeper we dug the warmer it was. Unbelievable.

At dusk, our suspicions were confirmed; the voice of Pacaya was the sound of volcanic eruptions. In the darkening sky, we saw a powerful sight, which none of us had ever witnessed. Red fireworks were exploding out of the crater from the active twin. A pyroclastic blast was depositing red-hot rocks on Pacaya's flank.

Later that night, after again contemplating George's words, *Go to the edge and look into the crater,* I asked my companions, "Who wants to get a closer look and check it out?" Amalia, the only other American, and Francois were game. We headed across a saddle between the two summits. The distance between the "twins" was about three-quarters of a mile. In my hand I carried my backpack as a potential shield. My thought was, *Something is better than nothing.*

The three of us walked across desolate terrain and began climbing the rock-belching twin. Surveying the scene closer, we saw that the active twin was covered with solidified lava rocks, which made hiking awkward. Fortunately, there was also a long sandy tongue hanging out of the crater's mouth. The tongue could provide a quick and easy escape route. It would be perfect for an, *"Oh my God! We're going to get eaten! Let's flee!"* running dash down the mountain.

About every ten minutes, a 20-30 second eruption blasted out of the crater and dropped glowing red-hot rocks called tephra. As I continued upward, Francois and Amalia began to cautiously lag behind. I stopped climbing at the perimeter of the falling tephra, and from there I could see that the rocks were golf-ball sized or smaller. A few minutes later, Francois and Amalia hiked up. We stood together at the perimeter and watched a series of eruptions. Amalia and Francois remained outside the area of falling red rocks—I pressed on.

I was no longer bolstered by George's words or my flimsy shield, but was encouraged by the eruptions I had observed. For hours I had been hearing Pacaya's voice, and I had been intently watching the volatile twin since sunset. There was a *pattern* to the eruptions. The timing of the eruptions, the landing zone, and size of the red-hot rocks had been consistent.

In synch with the volatile twin, I too developed a pattern as I moved up the mountain. When I heard Pacaya's voice start to roar and saw the glowing rocks fall from the sky—I immediately stopped. Then I watched the sky and held my ground. My backpack/shield remained at my side, ready if needed. Looking up, I hoped to never see or feel a baseball, basketball or Volkswagen size rock. Volcanologists call these larger projectiles "bombs" and "blocks." All the falling rocks continued to be small. The closest one landed ten feet away. Instinctively, I flinched and turned a shoulder to dodge another, but it wasn't necessary.

Between eruptions— fueled by adrenaline, excitement, and fear— I sprinted up the mountain. Breathless, I reached the crater's edge, where I stood awestruck, looking into the raw guts of the Earth.

Inside the crater was an orange-red ring of molten lava. I stared at the ring. There was a ring because the pool of liquid-lava was covered by a thick black capstone, like the lid of a pot. Alive—the capstone pounded and pulsated up and down. It beat like a heart.

My heart almost burst with the next eruption. Red-hot rocks blasted out. Enough pressure had built under the thick capstone that the force lifted its edge, like the lid on a pot when it boils over. Except the material wasn't boiling out—it was exploding. Rocks flew over and around me, as though I were inside a fireworks display. Pacaya's voice was in my face and *screaming*. It was difficult to hold my ground as glowing rocks hurled towards me. I stood on the sentient volcano's sandy tongue ready to flee.

When the eruption stopped, my screams were primal and involuntary. The air was thick; I could taste it. It coated my face, as I gagged on Pacaya's toxic sulfuric breath.

I watched a series of eruptions and then scrambled down to Amalia and Francois. "You have to hike to the edge and look into the crater!" They were reluctant yet willing, and we climbed to the crater's edge. The three of us stood together holding hands, with Amalia in the middle. Then the volcano erupted. Francois dropped Amalias' hand like it was on fire and fled down the sandy tongue.

I held Amalias' other hand for support, not restraint, and kept yelling, "It's okay, check it out! It's okay, check it out! It's okay, check it out!" I didn't quit yelling until the eruption stopped. Then we were erupting ourselves, uncontrollably screaming and jumping up and down.

We had to get Francois. He had run only partway down the tongue of sand. Francois was apprehensive but found his courage. The three of us again held hands on the edge of the crater, but this time with Francois tucked between Amalia and me. When the fury exploded, Francois stood firm.

Following a series of eruptions, we *had* to get our other friends. The three of us hiked down and yelled across the saddle. We insisted, almost begged them to join us. Only one British man stayed behind, but not my new friend David. Together, the nine of us hiked to the crater's edge and watched the Earth wake up and come to life.

After we returned to the sleeping summit, the group couldn't stop talking about Volcan Pacaya. One of the German women said, "Before we joined you, we could see your silhouettes on the edge of the crater. It looked like you were standing in a firestorm."

Rena, the sole Canadian, said, "I now understand how ancient people would think the Earth is alive."

When we left San Vicente de Pacaya the bus was full. To the chagrin of the driver, the ten of us climbed on top. David is in tank-top, with Amalia next to him. Francois and Rena are the two wearing sunglasses and sitting next to each other.

David and author with Volcan Pacaya in
the background. Sleeping summit is the left
peak, erupting summit is the right peak.

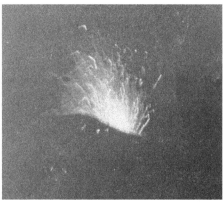

Poor image of the erupting summit, taken
from the summit where we slept.
Photo by David.

Photo of paper bill with quetzal on it.

Close Calls in the Sandbox

If the vast ski resorts of Europe were a sandy beach, the tiny and inconspicuous ski area of Les Collons, Switzerland, would be a child's sandbox. Some ski areas in Europe are so large that they have a seemingly infinite number of ski lifts. Many of those giant resorts are connected, creating mega ski complexes. Near Les Collons is the famous and huge ski area/station Verbier. Verbier and three large ski areas are collectively called The Four Valleys. Les Collons is on the perimeter of the four ski stations, but is so insignificant that the map of the four large ski areas cuts off half of Les Collons. Despite its small size, a human being on the ski mountain of Les Collons is as miniscule as a single grain of sand in a child's sandbox.

Many years ago, when one faced the Les Collons ski area from the base lodge, the left side had one chair lift, which served advanced and expert terrain. The right side had another chairlift, eight simple surface lifts, and a very old four-person gondola. Between the two sides was a steep section of cliffs—with no established ski runs. A skier could move from the left side to the right side on a low-angled ridge above the cliffs.

In 1989 I was in Les Collons for two weeks, working as a camp counselor/ski instructor, teaching teenage students on winter break from private prep schools in England. Our group of eight counselors taught every day, but occasionally, we would have a morning or afternoon off to free-ski. One afternoon, while free-skiing without students, I saw a paraglider setting up above the cliffs. He was only minutes away from launching. I stopped to watch, along with a handful of other skiers, and a fellow instructor, Deb, who was with her class.

At that time paragliding was an emerging sport, a novelty in Les Collons. The activity can be compared to sky diving, but with differences. A paraglider pilot launches from the ground and a sky diver jumps out of an airplane. The chutes/canopies have different shapes. Paraglider pilots control their flight by steering the canopy, and a skilled one may gain thousands of feet in altitude, if he successfully captures rising air currents.

The pilot had his bright red, yellow and orange canopy meticulously laid out on the snow. He had carefully untangled two dozen long nylon lines, which connected the canopy to his seat-harness. He was strapped into his harness, facing into the wind, and ready to fly.

The launch started when the pilot flicked his wrists and raised his arms, which lifted the nylon canopy a few feet off the ground. His canopy filled with wind and became "heavy." He struggled to move forward. Then the canopy took aerodynamic shape and raised itself skyward. The pilot continued moving, but now faster and less labored. Finally, he was running as fast as possible down the snowfield, headed toward the cliff edge.

Airborne! The launch appeared successful and the glider disappeared out of sight below the cliff. A normal flight would last about twenty seconds before the paraglider would reappear over the landing zone. The landing area was a large flat snowfield a short distance beyond the base of the cliffs.

Nobody watching the launch went anywhere. I held my breath, and subconsciously counted seconds. We waited one long minute. Two minutes, still no paraglider. Three minutes can feel like an hour, and after the agonizing third minute passed it was obvious the pilot had crashed.

The pilot had run down a slope which was about eighty yards wide at the top. Slowly, I skied down the right side of it. The snow was hard and wind-packed. I stopped at a rock outcrop and tried to peer over the edge. Deb, my fellow camp counselor/ski instructor, skied partway down the left side of the slope hoping to see the pilot. Her students waited. A steady wind and the distance between us made communication difficult. But with hand and arm gestures, we made it known to each other that neither of us could see the canopy or pilot. I skied towards Deb, who was still well above me. From my new vantage point I could see the snow didn't end at the edge of the cliff, but continued through a gap. I yelled at Deb, "I'm going to look for him!"

Cautiously, I began descending the vein of snow—a couloir—which became steeper and narrower. Uncertainty and concern filled my mind. I was worried about the pilot, and wondered what condition he would be in if I found him. I was also concerned about the couloir. Where was the snow leading me?

My home base that winter was the mighty Chamonix, France. A place where people climb and ski the "impossible" and ski tracks mark the mountains everywhere. But in the sandbox of Les Collons—I had never seen tracks, or people, heading into or out of this section of cliffs.

Would the couloir continue to steepen, transitioning into extreme terrain, the no-fall-zone? The no-fall-zone is a slope so steep that if one falls it can be difficult or impossible to stop. My other concern was that the line of snow would end above a tall cliff. The combination of extreme terrain with a cliff below is a nervous situation, with potentially bad consequences. If the couloir ended at a cliff, I could carefully remove my skis and climb back up, hopefully. At least Deb had seen me ski out of sight and knew where I had gone.

The couloir was shaped like the top half of an hourglass. It continued to narrow and get steeper. I carved prudent, solid, journeyman turns, combined with snappy hop-turns, and utilitarian side-slipping. My eyes constantly surveyed the snow immediately in front of my skis and down the couloir, while looking everywhere in hopes of spotting the pilot. Tall, gray rock walls flanked the thin white line of snow; the couloir was impressive.

Downward I went. The walls continued to tighten together. I approached the narrowest place yet, a choke. It was less than ten feet wide. Like a grain of sand I squirted through the waist of the hourglass. Once past the choke, the couloir became wider and less steep—and I saw a safe line to the bottom. But I felt only some relief. Where was the pilot?

A few more turns and I saw the bright canopy. And there was the pilot! He was sitting on the rocks at the side of the couloir, packing his paraglider into its large duffle-bag carrying case. I skied down to him. He greeted me with a smile and wired wide eyes. The pilot was glad to see me; I was thrilled to see him. He looked shaken but uninjured; no doubt his flight had been harrowing.

"Bonjour," we exchanged. We didn't speak the same lan-

guage but shared a few common words. From our simple conversation, which was more hand gestures than words, I felt almost certain that he was okay. The pilot had nearly completed packing his glider. I kept my skis on and sat on the snow while he finished. I wanted to watch him start down the couloir, to make sure he was solid on his feet, before I skied away. After his first steps the pilot began running, and then he leaped and bounded down the snow. Certain he was fine, I skied away. We both shouted "*Au revoir*!"

Right away, I looked for Deb and her gaggle of teenagers on the slope of Les Collons. When I located them, Deb gave me a huge hug. She and her students were really curious about the pilot and asked what had happened. I told them, "When I found the pilot, he was unhurt. And I don't know why he crashed." We talked a little more and I mentioned to Deb, "The couloir was an amazing place to ski. If I get time off, I want to ski it again. Next time it'll be a lot less stressful."

～

Four days later I had the morning off, and skiing the hourglass couloir had been on my mind. Five inches of dense snow had fallen overnight. It was the first new snow Les Collons had seen in weeks. I was confident the old snow was "solid"—free from avalanche danger and safe to ski. But what about the new snow?

Heading up the ski mountain, I rode the chair lift alone and pondered the snow conditions. Had the new snow securely bonded and attached to the old snow, making the couloir okay to ski? Avalanche forecasting is a science, but an inexact science. An incorrect forecast could have big-time ramifications. An untrue, but sad cliché among avalanche forecasters: *There are no living avalanche experts.*

I skied away from the lift, headed to the hourglass couloir. At the top of the couloir I skied down a small ridge, next to, but just outside of the hourglass. The ridge wasn't dangerous, because it was low-angled and the wind had blown away the new snow. I stopped at the right edge of the couloir and looked at the new snow. Was it safe to ski?

I estimated the new snow was five or six inches deep, with possibly a little additional snow blown-in. Many skiers love to ski fresh, untracked snow, including me. The new snow in the couloir looked like it would ski well. Hard wind can ruin good snow, but the surface had only slight ripple marks from a light wind. My mind continued to ponder and analyze. The couloir was an incredible place. I wanted to go. I debated for minutes. Only two choices, go or no.

My past back-country experience, combined with my intuition, said no. I didn't trust the new snow. I was okay with the decision to resist temptation. It was time to move on and enjoy the fresh snow and my morning off. How to get out of there? Two choices: I could remove my skis, shoulder them, and hike up the safe line where I had just skied. Or, I could opt for a faster and easier line. This was to leave my skis on and side-step uphill, while traversing across the new snow in the top part of the hourglass couloir. I chose the easier line.

The perimeter of the hourglass had no new snow because the wind had blown it away. But the center might have had up to eight inches on top of the old firm snow. My plan was to stay in the shallow part of the new snow, where it was only one or two inches deep. I *did not* want to venture into the deep snow. I entered the edge of the hourglass and started to traverse uphill. My skis cut and sliced the new snow, which was only an inch deep. I moved further into the hourglass. A few more shuffles of skis and the snow was two inches deep. I continued to side-step uphill and move forward. Now fifteen yards into the hourglass, the snow was two or three inches deep.

Suddenly, without a sound, I saw a crack open in the snow. It started at the tip of my leading ski. Instantly the crack zipped across the entire hourglass. I stood still, but my mind screamed *Avalanche!*

The snow *above* the crack— and where I stood— stayed in place. The new snow *below* the crack started to avalanche, it was sliding on the surface of the firm old snow. The two layers, old snow and new snow, had not bonded together very well. All the fresh snow *below* the crack was in motion, gaining momentum, and moving faster and faster.

The avalanching snow was shallow at first, only inches deep. But the tall, gray rock walls acted like a funnel. The mass of sliding snow became crushingly deep, powerful, and deadly when it converged and compressed into the narrow waist of the hourglass.

I stood still—with my skis planted solid on the firm old snow. I had not been swept away, knocked down, or even jostled. Like the paraglide pilot who crashed, I too was wide-eyed.

The avalanche quickly disappeared down the couloir, reminiscent of the way the paraglider pilot went out of sight after he launched. But seconds later, 600 vertical feet below, the avalanche reappeared racing across the flat terrain below the cliffs. The lethal mass was dense, heavy, and yards deep when it raged out of the hourglass couloir.

The mountains don't know who we are, nor do they care about us. Reading my journal years later, I was reminded that I called my parents that night for the first time in weeks. I never said a word about the avalanche. But I wanted to talk with someone who did care.

On a "small" mountain in the Swiss Alps, two grains of sand had close calls in the sandbox of Les Collons.

Google Earth image of Hourglass Couloir, marked by white circle.

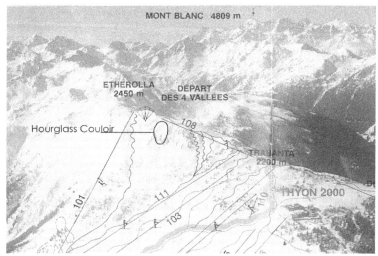

Les Collons trail map with circle around the Hourglass Couloir.

Mr. and Mrs. Midget

*(Literary license has been taken with the
first part of the story, including some fiction.)*

"... happy birthday dear Batman, happy birthday to you."
a chorus of friends sang out. The festive celebration took
place on Murphy's Hogback, at the Island in the Sky District of Canyonlands National Park, in Utah. I didn't hurry
to blow out the candles on the chocolate cake topped with
coffee frosting and scrumptious strawberries, a favorite. Instead I enjoyed watching the candles melt into short nubs
and tiny pools of red wax. At times, the Utah desert feels like
a hurricane but without the deluge of rain. We were loving
this windless night, but I decided to wait and see if a slight
puff of breeze might do the job for me.

Everyone sitting around the campfire was wearing
shorts, and all the men and the lone boy, Robbie, were shirtless. The fire was solely for ambience. Wood fires were illegal where we were camped, so Maggie, my girlfriend of
many years, brought manufactured logs of compressed and
glued wood chips. The early September night was moonless,
gorgeous, and star filled. Birthday or not, anyone could almost reach up and pluck a star out of the sky, hold it in their
hand and make a wish.

Marco handed me a gift-wrapped package. I held it,
shook it, smelled it, licked it, turned it upside down and

shook it some more, pretending I was trying to figure out the contents. With more enthusiasm than a hyped-up kid on Christmas morning, I shredded the wrapping paper. "A blender! I've always wanted a blender!" I exclaimed. It was the same old avocado green, thirty-year-old, heavy piece of non-working crap that my friends and I had occasionally given back and forth to each other over the last decade and a half.

~

Hard to believe, but I hadn't wanted to go to the desert for my birthday. Over the past several years Maggie and I had spent all our valuable vacation time with groups of friends, mostly on multi-day river trips. I was looking forward to a simple quiet trip with just the two of us, and I was hoping to see a new place. We had talked about it. Maggie knew how I wanted to spend my birthday. She knew how I felt.

Nevertheless, six weeks before my birthday, Maggie informed me, "I got a permit for a group of us to bicycle the White Rim Trail in Canyonlands. We'll be there over your birthday."

"But I thought we would..."

Stepping on my words, Maggie interrupted, "You love the desert and the White Rim Trail and you'll love everyone on the trip. Your good buddy Marco is coming, Steve and Diane (Maggie's best friends) are driving down from Wyoming with Robbie and Jean (their two children). Cindy is coming and so are..." All eleven people invited were close friends whom I really enjoyed, especially the two kids. The people on the trip weren't the problem.

Rather than follow our normal path to yet another ugly

and brain damaging argument, I simply used my hand to express my feelings. First I showed her the hand sign for "okay," with my thumb and index finger making an O. Then without moving any fingers I turned my hand around. The three remaining fingers—my pinky, ring, and middle finger—remained straight up and separated.

Do you think you know what I did next? Do you think I curled my pinky and ring finger down, and left my middle finger straight up by itself? No, I was done. The three fingers represented a W for—whatever. It was rare that I used the annoying Okay-Whatever sign, but the hand gesture said it all.

Sheepishly, Maggie whispered, "Cindy invited Princess Rea."

I *groaned*, "You mean, Gorgeous-Goddess-Groovier-than-God-Girl." I had been on trips with the princess before, and her self-absorbed nature was hard for me to stomach. I couldn't help myself and again spoke using my hand. For the first time ever, I silently flashed a second Okay-Whatever.

When I did open my mouth it was to calmly say, "Perfect. I know who I'm driving to the desert with—Marco. You can ride to the Island in the Sky with Cindy and the princess." Marco was like a brother, and lately we hadn't been able to spend much time together.

An hour later, alone, I popped my birthday-balloon full of bad attitude. First I had a talk with myself, out loud. "Mark, dealing with people—who feel like a pesky pain in the butt—is part of living." Then I chided myself a little for being a bit of a spoiled brat. While another group trip on the White Rim wasn't my first choice, I was lucky to be going on vacation over my birthday and revisiting a great place with a few close friends. I also encouraged myself not to let the negativity orbiting around the self-centered princess foul my world. Then, I started to get excited about going to the desert.

~

The White Rim Trail is a four-wheel-drive loop road, one hundred miles long. There are many miles of easy level road on white sandstone, the White Rim Sandstone Formation. The loop can be traveled in either direction. Both the start and finish of the ride are steep, because they're at the top of a 400-foot-tall layer of Wingate sandstone. In most places the Wingate Formation is a vertical cliff, miles and miles long. But nature has eroded the Wingate Wall and cut a pathway down the cliff face at two spots, the Mineral Canyon Road and Schaefer Trail. Both are dirt roads. The two roads are the beginning, and/or end, of the ride.

Before the Mineral Canyon Road and Schaefer Trail were constructed, ancient people probably traveled up and down at those places to access the Colorado River. Much later, cowboys scratched out trails there to move cattle. And in the 1940s or '50s uranium miners carved out the two steep, narrow, and precarious roads.

From the top of the Wingate Wall, the White Rim Trail drops 1200 vertical feet and passes through the Chinle and Moenkopi Formations before it reaches the White Rim Formation. Wingate Sandstone is found many places in the desert. But in some areas erosion has washed away all of the Wingate Sandstone or it was never originally deposited. Because of its tall cliffs, the Wingate Wall is one of the easiest layers to recognize. Occasionally, in the transition zone between some Wingate and none, there are tall towers of the pale-reddish-brown sandstone. Standing alone, those remnants of the Wingate Wall are spectacular formations. We'd be biking past a few, like Candlestick Spire and Airport Tower.

The eleven of us would use one pick-up truck, an old two-tone green and white Ford, to carry all the camping gear, food, and water. Once on the trail we planned to take turns driving and preparing group meals. Everyone would bring a mountain bike, except six-year-old Jean. She had a pink Barbie bike.

A permit is required to spend the night in Canyon-lands National Park. In the evening we planned to stay in designated camping areas, with names like Potato Bottom, Gooseberry Canyon, and White Crack. Along the White Rim Trail are eight designated camping areas, and each area has two to four campsites for groups like ours. Each campsite is numbered. The Park Service reserves the campsites and writes them on the permit. That way there's no confusion about where each group is camping. The sites are generously spread out. There's nothing worse than camping in heaven with neighbors from hell.

A nasty argument is like a malodorous mouthful of bad breath— it fouls the air and unpleasantly lingers. It's also bad for romance. Maggie and I had once again patched up our tiff and we drove to the desert together. The princess drove alone and stayed at a motel in Moab, Utah, the night before the trip. The morning of the rendezvous, at the Island in the Sky Visitor Center, everybody was on time—except the princess. When she finally arrived an hour-and-a-half late, she lamely said, "I know how these trips are. Someone is always late. Plus a girl needs her beauty sleep and I needed a big breakfast at my favorite diner in Moab." I was tempted to speak using my hand.

While we waited for the princess, ten-year-old Robbie was like an excited thoroughbred on race day. He wasn't chomping at the bit but he was stomping on his pedals, and he spun them in dizzy revolutions. Racing in circles, Robbie launched his bike off any rock or mound he could find.

After loading the princess's exceptionally large pile of junk into the bed of the pickup, I stroked her galaxy-sized ego, rather than nudge her off the Wingate Wall. I suggested to her, "Rea, you've been on the White Rim Trail many times, could you please lead us down Schaefer Trail? Oh, by the way, we're camping at Airport Tower." I said this while holding the back of Robbie's cycling jersey. Then I moved my other arm around his chest and gave him a one armed bear-hug—and didn't let go. As Rea dashed down the trail, I quickly unclipped Robbie's helmet before he could squirm away and race off with the princess.

Robbie scowled at me like I was the biggest jerk in the world. Then I asked my friends, "Please wait for me just a few more minutes." I feigned fumbling with my gear, retied my shoes, adjusted my biking gloves and futzed around. I knew the princess, if we gave her a brief head start she'd be out of sight until lunch or maybe even until we reached camp.

~

Motherly Advice: *If you don't have anything good to say*

about someone, don't say anything. I truly wish I could say the princess had an epiphany in the desert and became a saint—but she didn't. With my mom's words in mind I'll spare you some of the dirty details, but Rea only added to her growing reputation. When we asked her to help drive the old Ford, she refused. Cycling was fun, driving wasn't. Lunch is the simplest group meal to prepare, and Maggie had asked the princess to bring a lunch for the group. "Lunch" was a box of granola bars, one bar for each person. Groan. We had extra food and we could drive. No big deal.

The most egregious offense was the night she became the, self-proclaimed, Mistress-of-Ceremony. For well over an hour, Rea pushed her presence on the group. She insisted on being the center of our eleven person universe, and persisted in leading everyone in a bunch of dull games that frustrated the kids and increasingly irritated the adults. Ugh. Graciously, no one silenced the princess or spoke to her with their hand. There were other irritating moments. We survived. None of it was that awful, but the cumulative effect...

Many of us have friends like the princess, whose lives are ruled by the "It's All About Me" mentality. A small dose of these people is bearable. But traveling together for days, or spending a lot of time with them can be trying. The princess is still a friend— because nobody is perfect— except, of course, Batman.

～

Robbie was a tough and determined kid from the mountains of Wyoming. He wanted to ride or push his mountain bike the entire one-hundred-mile trip, which he did. Jean, his six-year-old sister, rode most of the way on the front seat of her parents' old, but comfortable, Ford F-150. The White Rim has many miles of flat and easy road. When the terrain and weather were little-kid-friendly, Jean's pink Barbie bike, complete with a white wicker basket, sparkly handlebar streamers, black-and-white training wheels, rubber-ball horn, and pink seat was lifted off the stack of camping gear in the back of the truck.

With her Mom's help, Jean had dressed in a pink top and white shorts. Her shorts were now pinkish from playing in the red desert dirt. Diane tied the laces on Jean's white sneakers and handed her a pair of pink cycling gloves. Diane then clipped her daughter's white helmet, which was decorated with girly-stuff stickers, on top of Jean's curly blonde hair. Once ready, Jean sat on her bicycle (technically because of the training wheels it was a quad-cycle) and cheerfully started pedaling.

The morning of my birthday, Steve and Robbie, father and son, were ripping down hills and gripping brakes, hootin' and hollering, cranking and banking on the rollercoaster terrain south of Murphy's Hogback. Diane was steering the pick-up, following everyone in the group. She was both "mothering" and manhandling the beastly Ford. Or as she liked to call the well-used trusty truck, Old Furd. Jean and I were toddling along by ourselves and doing just fine— until we weren't so fine.

The terrain turned steeper, and the dirt road changed from packed solid to loose and slippery, little-kid unfriendly. I stopped for just a minute to do something, and Jean wobbled by on her four wheels. She crested the top of a little hill, and just as she started down I yelled, "Jean, stop! Wait for me!" Too late. It wasn't exactly like a train wreck, but I could see the crash coming. I watched as Jean pressed her coaster brakes with all of her forty-five pounds and spindly legs. She did everything she could to slow down.

The crash was quick and thankfully not high speed. As soon as the Barbie bike got sideways, training wheels or not, Jean tipped over. She slid on the dirt to a mean stop. Ouch. Falling off her bike had to be scary. "Little-Girlfriend, are you okay?" I asked. Jean's face contorted and worked hard to hold back tears. She managed a nod, but little tears couldn't help but weep out.

Old Furd crested the hill behind us. "Mom!" The dam burst. Tears flowed like a flash flood. When you're six years old, calling 911 means almost nothing. Mom is the "number" you want when you've got a serious problem. Diane was the medicine for her young daughter's mind, the "finger in the dike," and Jean calmed down.

Getting back on the pink saddle: As it turned out, Jean's fall was more frightening than injurious, but I would have understood if she didn't want to ride her bike. Diane coaxed her young daughter, "Come on Jeannie-Girl, let's get on that pink pony and take it for a little ride. Just the two of us. Just you and me." Diane convinced Jean to ride a tiny bit farther. Quickly, before Jean could change her mind, I unloaded Diane's bike and chucked mine on the pile of stuff in the back of the truck. I didn't bother to secure my bike, they weren't going far.

Diane finished dusting off her daughter and unruffled Jean's pink and white attire. Together, mother and daughter rode about one hundred healing yards. I didn't even start the truck until Diane got off her bike and waved at me. I cruised up to them; bikes were shuffled, Diane got behind the wheel and Jean snuggled.

The roughest part of the White Rim Trail is the climb up Murphy's Hogback. It's actually not too terrible of a climb, except for one nasty sandstone step near the top. (A hogback is a sharp ridge with steeply sloping sides.) If you're driving, you want to bump into the rock-step with the right amount of speed and forward momentum. Too much speed and you'll smash the underside of your vehicle. Not enough speed and you'll stall the engine in a bad spot on a steep hill, with a drop off on your left that you don't even want to think about.

At the base of the climb up Murphy's Hogback, Steve was off his bike and sitting in the shade of a large boulder waiting for the truck. Diane and Jean drove up to him and stopped. Robbie had already started pushing his mountain bike up the long steep switchback.

Diane said to her husband, "Honey, you want to drive, don't you?" Steve just smiled. She added, "Old Furd is your baby, its best if you baby her up this monster hill." Diane slid over and Jean hopped across her mom's lap and sat between her parents. Jean could sense the subtle nervousness in the air and squeezed in tight to her dad and pulled her mom closer.

Steve told her, "Relax Jeannie-Girl, this *really* is going to be fun. It'll be a little like the bumper cars at the amusement park."

I was walking my bike up the switchback and stopped just a few feet below the ugly sandstone step to watch the action. As the green and white rig crawled by, and just before the truck hit the steep step, I heard Steve's voice out of the driver's side window, "Hang on girls. Here we go!" I had a perfect view of the Ford when Steve pressed down on the gas pedal at the right instant and bounced the front tires up the steep step. Loose rocks shot out behind some of the tires, as they spun and searched for purchase. Traction was found, as rubber bit and rolled up the vertical step.

Everyone else in our group was watching the Ford from on top of Murphy's Hogback. Loud cheers, shouts, and clapping erupted when Old Furd crested the switchback. Even the princess was there, yelling and celebrating.

At the end of the day we were camped at Murphy's Camp, high above the White Rim Formation. The site was perched on a small mesa along the hogback. The view was stupendous. Most notable, well off in the distance to the southwest, were two large colorful buttes and several tall rock spires.

Because it was my birthday I was excused from all tasks. Maggie and I were sitting together enjoying a cloudless sunset. Jean was hanging with us; she called us the M and M's, like her favorite chocolates. The two of us were marveling at the immense vista, and Jean was sitting at our feet scratching at the reddish-brown ground with a juniper twig. After Jean wandered back to the camp-kitchen, I looked down and she had written J-e-a-n in the dirt.

Maggie and I had our lawn chairs—and our minds—side by side.

Maggie said what I was thinking, "That must be The Maze way over there. Have you ever been to The Maze?"

"No, but after reading Edward Abbey's book *Desert Solitaire*, I've been intrigued by the place. I've wanted to go to The Maze for a long, long time." I answered.

"Me too. I've never been there either. It's been high on my list for as long as I can remember."

Maggie grabbed the small Canyonlands map that the Park Service had given us at the start of the trip. We oriented the map, and I said, "Those pinnacles way over there must be The Land of the Standing Rocks. And a little farther to the west are Ecker and Elaterite Buttes. I bet those small dark humps are the Chocolate Drops."

Maggie looked at the jumble of twisted canyons and sandstone fins, "I can see how it got its name, it looks like a maze. From what I remember when reading *Desert Solitaire*, parts of The Maze are inaccessible without a rope. Plus there are very few signs and no trail markers. What a remote place. No wonder Abbey loved it." She sighed, "Sometime I want to explore that part of the desert."

"Me too."

"Where do you have to be when we get off the White Rim trip?" Maggie asked.

"Nowhere. I don't have to get back to work for a few more days."

"Neither do I," she said.

In silence, both of us gazed at The Maze. Then Maggie turned and looked at me. "Are you thinking what I'm thinking?"

"That we're going to the Maze after this trip?" I asked.

Maggie just smiled and nodded.

"I can't believe it. We're going to The Maze. What a gift."

"Happy birthday, Mark."

～

(No more literary license)

Two days after a light puff of wind blew out the birthday candles, our group pedaled and grunted our bikes up Mineral Canyon Road to the end of the White Rim Trail. The trip had been great. At the end of the trail heartfelt hugs were exchanged all around, just one of my embraces was given somewhat disingenuously.

Maggie and I then headed off on our own to find the keyway to The Maze, the Flint Trail. The Flint Trail is another one-hundred-mile dirt road, and many of those miles are just plain mean and tough. It's not a loop road, and I don't know where it starts but it dead ends at the Doll's House in The Maze.

The two of us had heard about the notorious Flint Trail. We knew that to negotiate the dicey road it was best to leave any vehicle we didn't want too roughed up at home. A reliable "beater" vehicle with four-wheel drive, high clearance, and preferably a short wheelbase would work best. Maggie's pick-up truck was another Ford, but it was brand new, less than three months old. It was an *awfully* nice ride for the Flint Trail.

Enjoying the new car smell, Maggie and I rambled easy miles on the Flint Trail until we got to a place where the trail had earned part of its reputation. We parked at the top of the Orange Cliffs, which are Wingate sandstone, and walked to the edge and looked down on the most treacherous section of the trail. The road switched back and forth down a cliff face and dropped hundreds of vertical feet in a series of tight hairpin turns. We were sizing up the road, and its life-ending drop-offs. We also tried to see if another vehicle was headed up, because there was no room to pass except in a couple of extremely tight corners.

Pangs of trepidation permeated the cab, as we started to descend the rocky dirt road. Thankfully we met no one along the way. From the base of the Orange Cliffs, we continued around Teapot Rock towards our camp at Chimney Rock. I hopped out of the truck numerous times to help guide Maggie. She's an excellent four-wheeler and would have been fine without any help. But it settled my nerves to do something, plus we were creeping along so slowly it was easy to jump out. Four eyes were better than two in some places, when she tried to see over the hood. Once again I found myself using my fingers and hands to speak. Fingers pointed left or right to guide Maggie, and when she was lined up on the best spot, both hands motioned her forward. We must have done this fifteen times.

On the way to camp we stopped and longingly looked south into Ernie's Country. Two dear friends had backpacked there for five days. They raved about the fragile crypto-biotic soil which was the deepest they had ever seen. Alive with microscopic life, the "crypto" was four inches tall. Exaggerating, the two had described the soil as "tall as a field of wheat." The backpacker's creed: *Take only pictures and leave only tracks,* did not apply in Ernie's Country. The pair had walked on rock or in washes, because a trail of footprints across the delicate soil would remain a scar for a generation or ten. Both are astute naturalists. They used their skills to locate water at a tiny intermittent spring to extend their stay. For Maggie and me, Ernie's Country would have to wait.

Our drive from the top of the Orange Cliffs to camp at

Chimney Rock was about twenty miles and took a little over four hours. We arrived at camp an hour before sunset. The only manmade object in sight was a 4-inch by 4-inch wooden post planted in the ground. Chiseled into the post was a simple, CHIMNEY ROCK CAMP.

The designated place to camp was on a large, flat, slickrock area. Red, softball-sized rocks, placed more or less in a forty-yard-diameter circle, marked where the National Park Service wanted people to camp. Setting up camp would be simple. Drop the tailgate to make a table, unfold two lawn chairs, pull a few things out of the truck, and lay down a tarp to sleep on. With the sun sinking, the tasks could wait. I grabbed three beers, one for Maggie and two for me, and we went for a walk.

We trekked a short distance on pristine, soft, red earth, and then decided to hike up a fifty-foot-tall hoodoo to enjoy the sunset and our beers. The desert has interesting geography, arches and windows, mesas and buttes, towers and standing rocks, hogbacks and hoodoos. A hoodoo is a short pile or plug of rock.

Quietly, we sipped away while enjoying a breezy, purple, orange, and pink sunset. Removing binoculars from my pack, we took turns eyeing the scenery. I especially liked looking at Murphy's Hogback, which was over a day's drive away but only twelve miles line-of-sight. The sun touched the horizon about the same time a blast of wind grabbed my big floppy hat and blew it off of my head. The gust dropped the hat at the base of the hoodoo, on the eastern side. We had hiked up the west side of the rocks, but the easiest way to get the hat was to hike down the east side. No problem.

I scrambled down a few feet and stopped above a four-foot vertical drop. The next move was going to be a long step down onto a small ledge. The shelf of dirt and rock was two-feet wide and two-and-a-half-feet across. It was also under-cut a little, and I couldn't see the backside.

I sat down and reached for the ledge with the toe of my shoe. After placing my foot on the ledge, I shifted it slightly and then put my other foot on the small piece of rock. With both feet on the ledge, I paused and looked for the next move. After deciding where to go, I stepped across a foot-and-a-half gap of air onto a big boulder. Maggie was getting ready to follow me. When I turned around to watch her make the move—my heart stopped. But my mouth worked.

"Don't come this way! There's a buzz-worm on the ledge! A rattlesnake!" A very surprised and upset Midget Faded Rattler, with its tongue licking the air and tail rattling, was coiled and ready to strike. The backside of the ledge was vertical rock and the twenty-inch snake was snug against the wall. "Maggie, Mr. Midget is really upset. He's scared silly and shaking his tail."

After several minutes and with five or six feet between us, Mr. Midget settled down and uncoiled. Before he started to go anywhere, I decided to get the heck out of there. But first, I snapped a quick photo of Mr. Midget.

When I'd first stepped onto the ledge, I must have come within inches of stepping on the startled reptile. Lucky for me the small guy decided not to fight.

Maggie found a friendlier line off the hoodoo. I picked up the hat and we walked back to camp. Because of Mr. Midget, both of us paid more attention than usual to where we placed our feet.

In dimming light Maggie heated dinner, while I walked

on the slickrock and looked for a smooth place for us to sleep under the stars. I found a nice spot, unfolded a tarp and laid it out. I started to pull a sleeping bag out of its stuff sack, but stopped when I saw something small in a niche in the rocks. The tan-colored thing was only nine feet from the tarp. "Darn." I whispered to myself and stepped away a few paces.

Speaking just loud enough for Maggie to hear, I said, "Maggie, guess who wants to sleep with us tonight?"

"Who?"

"Mrs. Midget."

"Who?"

"Mrs. Midget. Mr. Midget's wife."

"No."

"Yep, she's quietly coiled up and comfy looking. Come see her. Walk softly, you don't want to disturb Mrs. Midget and have her start shaking her tail."

"You're kidding."

"I'm not kidding. She's right there," and I pointed at her. Without upsetting Mrs. Midget, I silently removed the tarp and went back to the truck.

Standing around our tailgate-table I started to get the creeps. "Maggie, I've been a little fearful of snakes all my life. Whenever I see *any* snake it startles me. I've only seen four rattlesnakes in my life and every time it scares the beje-ezus out of me. Now I've seen two Midget Faded Rattlers in twenty minutes and almost stepped on one of them."

I began to work myself into a frenzy, partly for fun and dramatic effect, but somewhat seriously. "Maggie, I'm won-dering where Mr. and Mrs. Midget's children are sleeping. What about Grandpa and Grandma Midget? Where are the aunts and uncles, and the Midget cousins. What about the Midget's close friends, and…"

Finally I exploded, "Maggie! The Midgets are messing with me! I'm sleeping in the back of the truck!"

Which is where we slept.

The Maze with a view of hoodoos from camp.

Mr. Midget.

Mrs. Midget.

Porcupines

The Huntress

"Battie?"

Karma on Mount Wayah

The Huntress

Kathy and I were lying in our tent; the lime-green nylon door was unzipped and wide open. The hour was nearing midnight and we couldn't believe it was still light. The two of us were in the corner of the world where Alaska, the Yukon Territory, and British Columbia join together. Neither of us had ever ventured so far north. We had heard of "The Land of the Midnight Sun," but the thought of sunshine at midnight had always seemed hard to imagine. But here at 59 degrees north latitude and a week after the longest day of the year, June 21, the summer solstice, seeing was believing.

We were drinking up the last sips of twilight—intoxicated by the magic hour—the hour of the day when the sun's low-angled light sometimes creates euphoric illuminations. In the far northern latitudes the magic hour includes bonus minutes, because the sun arcs slowly across the horizon before gently dipping out of sight. This is unlike the lower forty-nine states, where the sun seems to dive straight down.

While headed to Fairbanks, Alaska, Kathy and I had detoured off the Alaska-Canada Highway to hike thirty-two miles of the historic Chilkoot Trail. The trail and its highpoint, Chilkoot Pass, have been famous in northern lore ever since the Klondike Gold Rush. In 1897 and 1898 thousands of prospectors stampeded to the gold fields near Dawson City, in Canada's Yukon Territory. An image of hundreds of miners lined up and headed over Chilkoot Pass is represented on one of Alaska's license plates.

~

Many of the gold miners traveled by ship to the port town of Skagway, Alaska, in 1897 and '98. The Chilkoot Trail begins a few miles from Skagway. Eighteen long and tough miles from the start of the trail is Chilkoot Pass, elevation 3550 feet. Chilkoot Pass is also the border between the United States and Canada. Entry into Canada was not a given—nor was it simple. On top of the pass the miners were met and stopped by the Northwest Mounted Police. (Years later the name was changed to the Royal Canadian Mounted Police.)

Conditions in the Yukon Territory were harsh, especially during dark frigid winters when temperatures hit forty degrees below zero, minus 40. (Minus 40 is the same temperature in both Fahrenheit and Celsius.) The province was remote and supplies were scarce to nonexistent. The Mounties wanted to make sure that the prospectors were prepared with all the required equipment and supplies. So before receiving permission to enter Canada and being granted passage to the gold fields near Dawson City, the miners' outfit was inspected.

A typical outfit weighed between 1000 and 2,000 pounds. The heaviest required item—a year's worth of food. In 1897, the cost of the equipment and supplies was about $300. But the expense of moving all that gear could be just as much or more. The miners hauled their supplies using a variety of creative methods, including hand-built packs, two-wheeled carts, and various pack animals, even cattle. Sleds were used in winter and pulled by women, men, dog teams and oddly, teams of goats. On flat terrain, some sleds were ingeniously rigged with an improvised sail made from a canvas tarp. Tinglits, the coastal Native Americans, had been traveling the trail and crossing Chilkoot Pass for generations. They also helped carry supplies. Basically, the prospectors used any method that worked and hired anyone available.

The toughest section of the trail was the final climb up Chilkoot Pass, "The Golden Staircase." The terrain turns very steep at the base of the pass and rises one thousand vertical feet in only a half-mile. The trail was too rocky and rough for pack animals. A towing device was constructed by an entrepreneur. His simple mechanism used a long cable and sturdy sled, which was pulled uphill by a gasoline powered drum that coiled the cable. The resourceful man charged two pennies per pound. Later, private companies built a couple of different tramways that covered longer distances and cost a nickel a pound. For those who couldn't afford or didn't want to spend the money, they simply slogged their gear, again and again, up the "golden stairs."

Once permission was given by the Mounties, gravity helped the miners because then it was all downhill, downriver, and across lakes to Dawson City. Dawson City, the fabled "City of Gold," is on the Yukon River—560 miles away. Traveling on water was the preferred way to move gear; it was much easier to float a ton of provisions rather than carry them. The route from Skagway to Dawson City was called The Overland Route, but ironically ninety-five percent of the journey was on water, either on lakes or rivers.

Thirty-two miles from the start of the Chikloot Trail is Lake Bennett. Near the lake are the headwaters of the Yukon River, the largest river in Alaska and the Yukon Territory. Boat travel to Dawson City would begin from Lake Bennett, once the frozen Yukon River thawed. (A few prospectors used boats upriver of Lake Bennett, but most did not because the river was too challenging.) Thousands of people wintered-over all along the Chilkoot Trail between Skagway and Lake Bennett. Tent cities and camps sprang up overnight. The largest settlement was at Lake Bennett, where an estimated 5,000 people waited for the river-ice to break up. Using local lumber, the prospectors hand-crafted an eclectic collection of boats: rafts, punts, scows, barges, canoes, double-enders, skiffs, junks, and catamarans.

On May 29, 1898, the ice broke and the race was on to stake claim to the most promising land. Hundreds of prospectors left that day. As the first to leave navigated the rough Yukon River, hundreds more lined the banks and watched. Thousands of people, with millions of pounds of gear, left the following day. Many boats survived the arduous trip to Dawson City, but other craft were quickly destroyed in the first few miles. Some of the flotilla was struck by disaster in the whitewater, because they were overloaded, poorly constructed, or mishandled by inexperienced boatmen. For those miners, who had toiled brutally hard and had already endured so much, this was heartbreaking.

On the drive to Fairbanks, three of us detoured to Lake Bennett, where Kathy and I planned to start a three day hike on the Chilkoot Trail. Our traveling companion, Danny, wasn't in the mood for the thirty-two mile walk, so he drove Kathy's 1966 Dodge Coronet to Skagway and waited for us. The dark green old Dodge was a classic. The car had belonged to Kathy's grandmother; it only had 35,000 miles and was in mint condition.

Kathy and I were hiking the Chilkoot Trail in the opposite direction traveled by the gold miners. We were walking from Lake Bennett to Skagway—trekking from Canada into Alaska. Our one and only climb, up and over Chilkoot Pass, would be easy compared to the trials of the gold miners. Traveling by foot into "The Great Land of Alaska" appealed to both of us. There's something extra special about reaching a unique destination on foot. Perhaps it's days, weeks, or even months of excited anticipation. Or maybe by moving slowly, one more fully absorbs the experience.

Today the Chilkoot Trail between Skagway and Lake Bennett is called the Klondike Gold Rush Park, and is sometimes referred to as "The World's Longest Museum." Part of the "museum" is a series of photos taken during the gold rush in 1897 and '98. Copies of the historic pictures are placed along the trail, exactly where the old photos were taken. Artifacts, like discarded rusting pots and pans, metal cans, and leather goods, are also visible along or near the route. Decaying log cabins are also part of the "museum." A short distance below the summit of Chilkoot Pass, Kathy and I saw heavy metal machinery that looked like it might be part of a towing device. An estimated 20,000 to 25,000 people crossed the pass during the gold rush.

Chilkoot Pass is still the international border—but now it's a border in the wilderness. On top of the pass, Kathy and I were not greeted by the Royal Canadian Mounties—or any officials. We were the *only* people there. The two of us were welcomed by spectacular views of Alaska. In the far distance we saw tall rugged mountains, which held beautiful icy-blue glaciers and whose lower reaches were carpeted with deep-green forests of spruce. The Alaskan side of the pass receives more rain than the Canadian side, which is in the rain shadow. We couldn't see the Pacific Ocean because of cloud cover, but on a rare clear day it would have been a sight to remember.

~

Camping with Kathy at twilight on the Chilkoot Trail: abruptly, the serenity of the magic hour was interrupted. Kathy ripped open the zipper of her sleeping bag, leaped up, and dashed out of the tent. She was dressed only in her underwear. In her hand was a loosely woven, maroon wool sweater—but she wasn't putting it on.

An unsuspecting porcupine had just ambled by our tent. Kathy pursued it and easily closed in on the hapless quilled critter. To my amazement, she started swatting the unfortunate porcupine again and again with her maroon weapon.

But why? Despite being covered with needle-like quills, aren't porcupines harmless? They don't attack, do they? And aren't they possibly the slowest moving mammal on four legs? Can't imagine trying to skin one, but are they good to eat? If you leave them alone, isn't everything just fine?

Moments later, Kathy—the huntress—returned puffing with pride. In addition to her bra and undies she wore a big smile. "What's going on?" I asked. Proudly, she held out her wool sweater for display. Entangled and captured in the maroon fibers were about twenty quills. Kathy removed a quill and handed me one of her prizes.

"Is there something you plan to do with your trophies?" I asked. "They don't look edible. Did you need a toothpick?

My Swiss Army knife has one toothpick and I'd share it with you."

"Earrings, I'm going to make earrings."

"Nice hunting outfit."

(Much of the historical information was found in two books, *Chilkoot Pass: The Most Famous Trail in the North* by Archie Satterfield, and *Klondike Women, True Tales of the 1897-1898 Gold Rush* by Melanie J. Mayer.)

Extra Bits

A porcupine was not the only animal Kathy and I encountered on the Chilkoot Trail. A mile into our hike, the two of us were walking in an expansive open meadow, when we were surprised by a moose briskly walking toward us— with its head down. There was not a single tree or cover anywhere. Neither Kathy nor I had ever seen a moose and it was the biggest animal either of us had seen in the wild. We knew they had a reputation for being "goofy," both unpredictable and potentially dangerous. The two of us stopped, stood still, and watched. As the massive mammal kept getting closer, our anxiety increased. Only twenty-five yards from us, finally, it lifted its head. We hoped it wouldn't be upset or panic, and drop its head and knock us over. Its rack of antlers was as wide as the front grill on the '66 Coronet. Without breaking stride, it deftly detoured around us.

~

List of items needed by the miners, which was distrib-
uted by the Northern Pacific Railroad:

Food:

200 pounds bacon, 400 pounds flour, 85 pounds assort-
ed fruit, 50 pounds cornmeal, 35 pounds rice, 24 pounds
coffee, 5 pounds tea, 100 pounds sugar, 25 pounds fish, 15
pounds soup vegetables, 50 pounds oatmeal, 50 pounds
dried potatoes, 50 pounds dried onion, 25 cans butter, 100
pounds beans, 4 dozen tins condensed milk, 15 pounds salt,
1 pound pepper, 8 pounds baking powder, 2 pounds baking soda, 1/2 pound mustard, 3/4 pound ginger, 36 pounds
yeast cakes, 60 boxes of matches, 5 bars of soap.

Clothing:

1 suit oil clothing, 3 pairs snag-proof rubber boots, 3
pairs heavy shoes, 1 dozen heavy socks, 6 pairs wool mittens,
3 suits heavy underwear, 2 Mackinaw trousers, 2 pairs over-
alls, 2 hats, 4 heavy woolen over-shirts, 1 Mackinaw coat, 1
heavy rubber-lined coat, suspenders, handkerchiefs, snow
glasses, 2 pairs of heavy woolen blankets, 2 oil blankets, 4
towels, buttons, thread, needles, 5 yards mosquito netting.

Equipment:

1 large bucket, 1 set granite buckets, 2 axes plus extra
handle, 2 picks, handsaw, whipsaw, 1 shovel, pack strap, 6
files, drawing knife, brace and bits, jack plane, hammer, 3
chisels, butcher knife, 200 feet 3/8 inch rope, 10 pounds
pitch, 5 pounds oakum, 2 caulking irons, 15 pounds nails,
tent, canvas, whet stone, compass, goggles, quartz glass,
quicksilver, 2 frying pans, coffee and tea pot, 40 pounds
candles, eating utensils: plate, cup, knife, fork, spoon, pots
and pans, steel stove for 4 men, gold pan, gold scale.

Additional items were also noted, such as: medicines, reading matter, guns, ammunition, and personal items.

An Alaska license plate with miners walking up Chilkoot Pass.

Historical photo of Chilkoot Pass with gold miners hiking up pass. Hegg, E.A (1867-1948) * Public domain. Photo from the Internet.

Kathy near the top of Chilkoot Pass wearing the maroon sweater.

Old handmade snowshoe.

"Battie?"

Addy is an up for anything, wild on life, go for it, Australian. Like a bellows stokes a fire, Addy's every breath fuels her fiery essence. A biologist by education, she is passionate about the outdoors, nature, and adventure. My girlfriend, Margie, and I met Addy on an eighteen-day, sixteen-person, 225-mile river trip through the Grand Canyon. Every day Addy would cover her nose, lips, and ear tops with some crazy combination of orange, yellow, blue, white, or pink zinc oxide to fend off the sun, so she could fully embrace the day. She never used just drab white.

Near the end of our trip, Margie asked Addy, "What are you doing after we get out of the canyon?"

"This down-under Sheila has not a flippin' clue." (I have no plans.) Addy answered.

Margie told her. "Come stay with Mark and me. It would be great to spend more time together."

To further entice Addy, I added, "You should see Colorful Colorado when it's not covered in snow." (Addy had only been to Colorado in winter.) "But beware of springtime in the mountains, it's wacky; it's both summer and winter. One day it'll be sunny, warm and beautiful. And the next day, hour, or even minute, it might pour freezing rain or dump a foot of snow. By the end of April, and especially May, most Coloradans are *way* over the snow. But sunshine or a whiteout, you'll love it."

"Tits up. You two are chummy cobbers. I'd love to hang at your shag-shack." (Great. You two are good friends. I'd love to stay at your place.)

~

Back home in Colorado, I told Addy I had the day off and asked her, "Do you want to hop on the back of my dirt-bike and go for a motorcycle ride? We can creep up the front of Aspen Mountain on Summer Road to the top of the ski area." Knowing Addy, I knew her answer before I even asked the question.

"Yeah Battie..." and she rattled off more Australian slang. Battie? My "mighty" and long time nickname, Batman, from an un-mighty and un-heroic childhood, had been reduced to Battie. The change from Batmale to Batman is easy to see. But now in Addy's quirky Australian language my name had become—Battie?

I kick-started the pleasant sounding, deep-throated, thump-thump-thumping, four-cycle, old-beater-dirt-bike. Addy approved, "Battie, I'm glad your motor bike isn't one of those yappie sounding, hyperactive, piss-ant and annoying bikes. You know, the ones with the high-pitched and whiny engines. The daggie ones."

"Yep, those screaming, ying-ying-yinging, two-cycle engines are hard to like."

Off we went, attired in sweatshirts, jeans, hiking boots and helmets, with no additional body armor. We had dressed for scenery, not speed. I also wore a pair of lightweight, inexpensive, white cotton work gloves with black rubber nubs for gripping.

Addy and I chugged our way up the front of Aspen Mountain on a steep dirt road. From the summit of the ski area, at over 11,000 feet, we followed another unpaved road across Richmond Ridge. The dirt two-track traverses an area dear to me, and like a person who intimately knows their driveway and backyard, I knew the terrain well. I had worked in the area for years as a ski guide.

Three miles across Richmond Ridge, Addy the biologist spotted a porcupine. It was the first she had ever seen. My ears rang and ribs winced when she banged my helmet and jabbed my chest. Addy had my attention. I stopped the faded red Honda so she could get a closer look. If I hadn't stopped, Addy probably would have jumped off. Together we followed the ambling quilled critter.

Addy exclaimed, "Oz has heaps of crawlies, bities and pokies. But no porkies!" (Australia has many things that crawl, bite, and sting, but no porcupine.)

I searched back in my memory, and remembered the time a friend had swatted one of the prickly beings with a sweater to get some quills. Hoping to stoke Addy's experience, I asked, "Do you want some quills?"

"Corker of an idea, Ace!" (What a great idea, excellent!)

I removed the white work glove from my right hand and walked to within five feet of the porcupine. Then I inched a little closer and threw the glove at the animal. My thought was that the porcupine would shake the glove off and a few quills would remain stuck to it. Wrong! The harassed critter simply kept waddling away. But now it was wearing a glove on its back.

My brain groaned, *You Idiot!* Upset by my poor decision and bad behavior, the unhappy porcupine cowered against a fallen log for protection.

(Years later I learned more about porcupines from the book titled, *A Naturalist's Guide to Canyon Country*, by David Williams and Gloria Brown.*)

> *"The hollow quills are modified hairs, loosely attached to the body. Porcupines cannot shoot their quills; when harassed, they swing their tail about, driving the spirally barbed points into an adversary."*

Feeling terrible, I wanted to right my wrong and remove the glove. I moved to within a foot of the frightened animal. Warily, I reached down with my bare right hand. Not knowing what would happen, I grasped the glove and gently pulled. The glove didn't budge. I adjusted my grip and pulled harder. Still no luck. The glove was stuck.

I let go and stepped away, relieved not to have quills in my hand and arm, or been bitten, or whatever porkies do when they're attacked. It was time to regroup. Meanwhile, Addy was doubled over laughing her Aussie arse off.

I spoke to her in her native tongue. "Don't wee in your knickers." (Don't pee in your pants.)

I muttered to myself, "Okay, okay, calm down, and try again." I didn't want to brutally rip the glove off, like a painful hair removal waxing. Again I reached down, grasped the glove, and started to pull harder and steadily. The quilled critter started softly crying, like a tiny infant.

---

*Williams, David - Illustrated by Brown, Gloria; A Naturalist's Guide to Canyon Country, 2nd Edition; 978-0-7627-80716; Guilford, CT; Falcon Guides; March 2013; Page 93.

Desperate, I pulled harder. And it cried much louder, like an upset toddler. "Damn," I mumbled and let go empty-handed.

The porcupine and I had had enough. I stepped away. It hurried off, and if porcupines could run it would have been sprinting.

Teasing me, Addy said, "No good onya for you, Battie. You look like a bit of a bounce and a dipstick." (No congratulations for you. You look a little like a bully and a fool.)

Addy's nickname for me now felt like a perfect fit. But only if it was spelled B-a-t-t-y.

Addy did speak using lots of entertaining Australian slang, but her quotes are nowhere near exact. I did a Google search of "Australian slang," one site had 500 words and terms.

Porcupine in the Utah desert.

Gloves.

Karma on Mount Wayah

Two hundred yards below the summit of Mount Wayah, out of the wind in a protected place, I wrestled with four layers of long-sleeved clothing in an attempt to see the end of my elbow. It's difficult to see the end of one's elbow and part of it is impossible to view without a mirror. I know this from my time as a house painter because it was a spot I often missed when cleaning up. Staring at my elbow—on the periphery of what I could see— I vaguely noticed a tiny dark speck. The speck was the size of the round part of this "a."

I thought the tiny thing might be a piece of dirt. So, in the way I sometimes get rid of a bug on my body, I flicked the dark speck with the back of my index finger. It didn't budge. Not sure if I had caught the speck with a good flick, I thumped it. The speck still didn't move, so I ran my fingertip across it. I didn't feel anything strange, but the speck didn't rub off.

~

This story is about two hikes. The first was with my sister-in-law Mary and my dog, five-year-old, Border collie mix, Mitianna. The three of us drove up a dirt road toward the summit of Sunlight Peak, which is near the city of Glenwood Springs in Colorado. At 10,625 feet, the mountain is the tallest in the surrounding area.

A locked gate blocked the road about a half-mile below

the summit, so we decided to park and start walking. Mary, Mitianna, and I followed the light-brown dirt two-track, which traversed back and forth across the mountainside as it continued to the top. The south-facing slope was awash in sunshine, and covered by groves of aspen trees and open meadows filled with abundant wildflowers.

It was mid-summer, and the flowers were in full bloom and stunning. Most seductive were the wild roses. Hundreds of roses, each with petals a subtle shade of pink and a bright yellow center, kept luring us in and slowed our ascent. Their fragrance was impossible to resist. "Just one more sniff," Mary and I kept saying each time we stopped and bent down and gently pulled another thin thorny branch to our faces. Our noses were dusted with tiny traces of yellow pollen and filled with *eau de heaven*. Mitianna's nose was interested in different smells—those associated with four-legged critters.

We reached the top of Sunlight Peak, which is level ground about a half-mile long and one hundred yards wide. The summit was once covered by a forest of spruce trees, but a large part of the mountaintop has been cleared and bulldozed flat. On the summit plateau are about a dozen tall metal towers, which had been constructed where the spruce trees formerly lived. Many of the structures were taller than the remaining trees, and I could only guess their functions. We heard sounds, but not the usual sounds of nature. The towers were abuzz with low volume beeps, drones, hums, ticks, clicks, and whirrs.

The three of us walked past the towers to the far end of the long flat summit. On a previous hike here, I had found a seldom-used trail that started at the edge of the plateau. We continued our walk on that trail and with our first steps found ourselves in pristine forest. Once in the woods, rather than another human, we were more likely to see a variety of wildlife, anything from a moose to a marmot.

Mitianna is loyal. The devotion she feels to her human pack is my favorite of her many good qualities. On our hike, Mitianna was off her leash but seldom more than a few yards away. Occasionally she wandered away, following her nose, but quickly returned. Mitianna always knew our location and we were hardly out of each other's sight. In a natural setting, when we are away from cars and other hazards that the Border collie doesn't fully understand, I almost never worry about her. Not once during our hike did Mitianna sprint off and run after any small critters.

My Border collie's prey-drive, the instinctive urge to chase small game like a rabbit, squirrel, or chipmunk, is her worst habit. This has been a concern and a problem along the road that runs by our house, and also in cactus-country. When she "sees red" and instantly chases after something, she's run full speed into a barbed wire fence and also been clipped by a car. I wish I could communicate better with Mitianna and explain the dangers of her behavior.

Mitianna doesn't chase large game, but gives them her classic Border collie stare. She crouches low, with her ears pointed straight up. Fully alert, she doesn't move a muscle but quivers all over, ready to explode. Her eyes are intense and unwavering. Border collies are working dogs that herd sheep and other livestock. People who work with the breed have said their stare is so powerful they can herd with just their eyes.

Our hike appeared uneventful. We sat in a sunny meadow and ate a picnic lunch, while enjoying an expansive view of mountains fifty-plus miles away. Mary took a few photos. Mitianna stayed by our side. Nothing unusual.

"Load up," I told Mitianna. Border collies are smart dogs and it's a directive the bright girl doesn't need, but I enjoy saying it out of habit. The three of us got into my blue-gray Toyota truck, Blue Eyes, which is short for "Blue Eyes White Dragon." My stepdaughter, Ivy, was a Pokémon and Yu-gi-oh devotee. When Ivy was young, she named both the truck and Mitianna after Pokémon and Yu-gi-oh characters. (Some readers with children might groan, "Ugh, please, not more Pokémon and Yu-gi-oh.")

On the backseat of Blue Eyes was an open duffle bag of clothes. Mitianna plopped down on the unzipped duffle, shifted about and nested into the bag of garments. The large collection of clothes lived permanently on the backseat and contained nothing dressy. Mitianna loved curling up there; it was her place in Blue Eyes. I turned the key and we headed home.

Later that evening Ivy, who is an animal lover, snuggled with Mitianna. Ivy let out a loud yelp when she got poked by something sharp in Mitianna's snout. Annie, Ivy's mom and my wife at the time, started checking Mitianna's face and muzzle. She found porcupine quills. Annie looked at Mary and me and asked, "Did either of you see Mitianna tussle with a porcupine?"

Mary and I were both surprised at the discovery of quills and I told Annie, "You know Mitianna, she's a faithful girl. She was hardly out of sight. Plus, Mary and I never even saw a porcupine."

Mitianna is extremely good natured and trusts the humans in her pack. She patiently allowed Annie to check her face and muzzle, and then remained mostly still while Annie removed about ten quills. Porcupine quills are like needles, and it struck me as ironic that the tool Annie used for the job was a pair of needle-nosed pliers. End of the story? No.

Karma could be described as: The law of cause and effect. How one's actions affect their future. Karma is a principal precept in the eastern religions of Buddhism and Hinduism. The concepts of reincarnation and past lives are also part of those religions. In both religions, how one acted in past incarnations affects this life and possibly future lives. Karma also applies to a person's current life: how one acts and what one does in this life—affects this life.

I've heard a western culture perspective of karma described as: *What goes around comes around. You get back what you give out.* Thinking back on two stories, *Mount Wayah* and *"Battie?"*, was a pot full of western-karma starting to simmer and thicken, and about to bite me because I had thrown a white cotton work glove at an innocent porcupine?

Karma could be described as: The law of cause and effect.

The second hike of this story took place nineteen days after walking to the top of Sunlight Peak with Mary and Mitianna. The odd adventure started when I drove Blue Eyes to a remote parking lot. The out-of-the-way spot is the trailhead to a series of lakes and is also the starting point to the summit of Mount Wayah. It's a peaceful place, around 10,000 feet above sea level. Parked there, I spent a comfy night in the back of Blue Eyes. I didn't sleep under the stars but under a sturdy fiberglass camper top, which covered the aptly named "bed of the truck." Plush carpet on top of a thick carpet pad, along with a hefty camp-pad on top of the two, softened the metal bed. Two sleeping bags, one zipped and the other unzipped like a blanket, guarded well against the cold night air at high altitude.

At first light, with an early-morning fuzzy mind, I started to multi-task. I packed for a hike to the summit of Mount Wayah, while mindlessly preparing and eating a simple breakfast. I dropped the tailgate, set up a small backpacking stove on the improvised table, and began heating water. While waiting for the water to boil, and still half asleep, I rummaged around in the ever-present duffle bag of clothes on the backseat of Blue Eyes. In dim light and not paying much attention, I started to pull out some of the appropriate clothes for the hike.

Breakfast was quick and utilitarian. Two big cups of instant coffee, black and simple, were the best part of an austere meal. Once the water was done heating, I was done cooking. I wasn't hungry, but began chewing a dry bran muffin and chomping on an apple; I ate only because my body needed fuel. But I was starving for coffee and its ability to warm my core and melt the fuzz in my head. I went back and forth between the tailgate table and the duffle bag of clothes, boiling more water and looking for additional clothing. Mechanically, while sipping and chewing, I gathered the last items of clothing and stuffed them into a daypack.

On autopilot and still sleepy, I began hiking within twenty-five minutes of first waking up. Slowly my brain engaged, as my body placed one foot in front of the other on an established trail. For an hour and a half I walked on the well-worn footpath, which paralleled the massive crest of the Continental Divide. Then I turned west, off-trail, and started to seriously huff and puff up the steep flanks of Mount Wayah.

Some days in the mountains, one's body or the weather says: *No summit for you today. Go home.* On that morning, thick, gray-black storm clouds were dashing at high speed over the divide. The mountains were not extending an open-armed welcome, but at least the blustery conditions hadn't given me a boot-to-the-butt and sent me home. My body felt good and was pushed upward by a motivated mind. I had summit fever. It was stronger than normal because of my mission to try and reconnect with Chris and the memory of his deceased dog, Wayah the Malamute.

If I got to the top, I had a plan. First I wanted to read the register on the summit and see if Chris had been back. If he hadn't, I planned to write down the names and home-towns of the people in the register to see who had been up the peak. Maybe a friend of Chris' had signed the log, and I could study it later and gain a clue to Chris' whereabouts. I also wanted to use my camera to take a couple of pictures of Wayah's photo. Chris had included a photo of Wayah with his handwritten page eulogizing his beloved dog. The plan also included writing Chris a new note and leaving it in the waterproof tube which contained the register.

My curiosity about Chris and Wayah had only grown since I'd first met Chris. While on a desert trip with a friend from Wyoming, I told him that I'd met an amazing long-distance backpacker. When I mentioned the names "Chris" and "Wayah" my buddy's eyes popped open. Not only had my friend and his family met Chris and Wayah, but they had given them a ride. Chris and his four-legged brother were at the end of a fifty-five mile, dead-end road, which terminated in the wilderness at a very isolated place in Wyoming. My pal tried to remember why the two needed a lift. He told me, "I can't be sure, but I think Wayah was having problems with the pads on his paws."

The hike to the summit, at just over 13,000 feet, went well. An added bonus was watching four bright-white, sure-footed mountain goats climb dizzy-steep terrain. The nimble footed four ventured to precipitous spots, places I would not want to tread without a rope.

As soon as I got to the summit, I excitedly leafed through the small notebook/register to see if Chris had been back. No luck, he hadn't. And no one who'd signed the register had specifically mentioned knowing Chris. Then I knew, I'd be on top of the peak for a while, writing Chris a new note and copying the register. Meanwhile, the weather hadn't gotten any nicer.

Sitting on the ground, I turned my back to the wind and stripped off two layers and a sweat-soaked tee-shirt. Brrr, I was down to bare skin. Remaining seated, I hurried and pulled all the clothes out of my daypack and started re-dressing. As fast as possible, still seated, I put on a long-sleeved tee-shirt and a thin layer of fleece and zipped it to my chin. Next, I put on the same sweatshirt I'd worn on the climb, then a nylon windbreaker and fleece vest. Lastly, I added a wool cap and a light pair of gloves, and quickly pulled up the hood of the windbreaker.

Ten minutes later, I phoned home to let my wife know I was okay and had reached the summit. I'd been sitting the entire time. I dialed, and then stood up and waited for Annie to answer. When I stood up, I experienced an odd feeling in my right elbow. "Hi Annie, I made it. I'm on top of Mt. Wayah. Darn, there's something wrong with my elbow. Sorry, let me call you back in a minute."

I flexed my arm a few times, and used my hand to check my elbow through four layers of clothing. My fingers didn't find anything, but my right elbow felt a little funny when I moved it. Then I wrestled with all the layers and tried to get a look. Nothing was obvious. I had cut my elbow three weeks earlier while kayaking and thought perhaps the injury might have something to do with the odd feeling in my elbow.

I redialed. "Hi Annie. Sorry about that, everything's fine. I don't know what's with my elbow. I'm seeing the doctor tomorrow for a check-up. I'll have him take a look." Annie is not a worrier, but I hated to call her from a remote mountain top and tell her I had a problem, especially since she knew I was hiking alone. The weather got meaner and began hitting me with small pieces of hard, hail-like snow. I hunkered down and focused on the tasks. While working, I ate a little lunch and tried to forget about my elbow.

An hour later it was time to head home. For the most part I had successfully forgotten about my elbow. But when I started walking—and put my arms in motion—my elbow definitely felt weird.

Two hundred yards below the summit of Mount Wayah, I found a protected place out of the wind. I dropped my pack and rolled up my sleeves to get a better look at the end of my elbow. That was when I barely noticed the tiny speck on the periphery of what I could see. So I had flicked the dark speck and then thumped it. But the speck refused to move.

I keep my fingernails cut short, but with them I attempted to pinch the dark speck. I needed to use my left hand because the speck was on my right elbow. My right hand has pretty good coordination, but my left hand stumbles around like a tanked-up drunk. Unsure—if I even had a grip of something that could be nothing—I slowly began to pull. Shockingly, the speck kept coming and coming and coming. I pulled out a broken porcupine quill, almost an inch long.

∼

I never saw the porcupine Mitianna tangled with, and never saw a quill on her. For nineteen days, I never saw the quill in my duffle bag of clothing on the backseat of Blue Eyes; the quill that had got there from Mitianna. Never saw the quill in any of the garments when I got them out of the duffle bag and packed them for the hike up Mount Wayah. Never saw the quill in my clothes when I pulled them out of the daypack and dressed on the summit. And I didn't feel much pain, when I stood up to call Annie and the quill went into my elbow.

∼

A sagely, older mentor once gave me some thoughts on karma: "In our society karma is a very misunderstood word and concept. Think of karma not as a debt to be repaid—but an opportunity for growth."

Is there karma? I like to think there's karma. And that during our long journey through life, big events or little things happen—things that change us. Hopefully for the better. Somehow, I like to think that the arrogant become humble, the selfish become generous, and that the cruel become kind. And those who throw a glove at wildlife—get a clue.

Was the porcupine quill in my arm, actually karma from my boneheaded glove incident? Perhaps, but who really knows? What I do know, is that when all the pieces of this story came together, this incident added to my belief that life is most unusual.

Extra Bits

David Thompson (1770-1857) is as well known and famous in Canada as Lewis and Clark are in the United States. In the early 1800's, Thompson and Lewis/Clark were exploring the western reaches of their respective nations. Lewis and Clark's Corps of Discovery was a two-and-a-half year journey. Thompson spent a *lifetime* exploring and surveying.

Thompson established trading posts in Western Canada and the Northwestern United States. Over his career, Thompson mapped over 1.5 million square miles and has been described as "the greatest land geographer who ever lived."

Sources of the River is an informative book written by Jack Nisbet about David Thompson's life and explorations. Nisbet occasionally uses direct quotes from David Thompson's field notebooks. Thompson wrote a total of seventy-nine books.

During David Thompson's explorations, food was sometimes very, very scarce. On one particular trip, one of Thompson's men became extremely sick and Thompson provided medical assistance. The paragraph below is from *Sources of the River*. I believe it was taken directly from David Thompson's field notebooks.

Beaulieu has been these ten days so very ill that he could not help us and at length so much so, that we despaired of his Life—his Complaint a violent Cholic and Pain under his ribs on the Left. This morning, perceiving a small Swelling close under his left Rib, mid of the side to be enlarging—he was feeling it with attention, and by his finger feeling something rough he sent for me. It appeared to be a small splinter—I extracted it and to our great surprise found it was a porcupine Quill, that had made its appearance from inwards, it was of the short thick ones on the Rump and Tail of the Porcupine. It can be accounted for only by supposing that when he eat part of the Dog (Thompson sometimes referred to horses as Big Dogs) the day we passed the Height of Land, he had in eating the Meat swallowed the Porcupine Quill in the Meat, as he is a voracious eater.

Towers on the summit of Sunlight Peak.

Mitianna and author on the day of the first hike. Photo by Mary Haug.

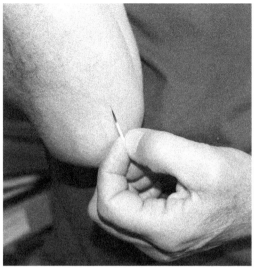

Not an actual photo of the day on top of Mount Wayah. Photo by Cindy Rogers.

Headwaters to Confluence

The grueling Ironman Triathlon, on the Big Island of Hawaii, starts with a 2.4 mile swim, followed by a 112 mile bicycle ride, and ends with a marathon-length run of 26.2 miles. The Ironman—which includes women—got me thinking. What about a triathlon combining skiing, biking and kayaking? With the idea of a quirky triathlon brewing in my brain, I called my good buddy, whom I sometimes refer to as Up-For-Anything-Sam.

"Sam, think about this. You and I can drive to the top of Independence Pass and from there we'll hike/ski-tour to the summit of Blue Mountain." (Independence Pass is 12,095 feet in elevation and Blue Mountain is 13,711.) "We can spend a few minutes relaxing on top of the peak and then ski Blue back to the car. From Independence Pass, we'll bike down Highway 82 to Aspen and have breakfast in town. After eating we'll keep biking down-valley to my house in Basalt. Then we can kayak the Roaring Fork from Basalt to Glenwood Springs. We'll finish in Glenwood, where the Roaring Fork River meets the Colorado River, at the confluence."

I could almost see Up-For-Anything-Sam's head nodding in agreement, as I continued talking into the phone. "Once we get to the top of Blue Mountain it'll be all downhill, down-road, downriver. Gravity will pull us all the way to the confluence, all sixty miles. Since Blue Mountain is the headwaters of the Roaring Fork River, we can call our full day The Roaring Fork Headwaters to Confluence Triathlon."

I asked him, "What do you think, Sam?"

"When are we going?"

~

Blue Mountain is by far my favorite peak to ski in the back-country; I think it's the combination of all the things that one doesn't have to deal with, plus a bonus thrown in. The peak is easily accessed on a paved road, no vehicle trashing. Route finding is all above timberline and straightforward, no being confused about which way to go or bashing around in the dark timber. No creeks to cross. Not arduously long and brutal, the summit is reachable in about two hours or less. Not super steep, which in the backcountry can be good for a lot of reasons. Once your skis are on, they stay on; there's no bare ground to cross. And the hike is all up, no giving away any vertical feet that you've climbed by yo-yoing up and down. Top to bottom the snow is usually very good, unlike some mountains. There's bonus skiing, an extra 600 vertical feet, because one doesn't have to ski back to their car but can ski to the highway well below. The views are in-credible and forever, and if any weather is coming it's not a surprise.

Perched high on the Continental Divide, Blue Mountain is also called Twining Peak. It's unusual for a mountain to have two names, but the topographical map of the area in-cludes both names. I have no idea why. As I thought more about it, I realized that Blue Mountain is on the county line between Lake and Pitkin County. The two counties are sepa-rated by the Continental Divide—a significant physical barrier. Maybe in the early days, before telephones and even telegraph lines, the people east of the divide started calling the mountain one name and the people west of the divide used a different name. Blue Mountain, Twining Peak... most people I know just call it "Blue."

Biking on Colorado State Highway 82 to Aspen is ripping good fun. The highway has a split personality. Above the famous ski town, located at 8000 feet, the highway is two lanes of narrow and twisting pavement, which is precarious in places as it climbs to Independence Pass. In one place called "The Narrows" it's actually only one-and-a-half lanes wide and doesn't have a painted double yellow line. For good reason, Highway 82 between Aspen and Independence Pass is restricted to vehicles less than thirty-five feet. Below Aspen the road is a heavily traveled four-lane highway which starts/ends in Glenwood Springs, where it joins Interstate 70. Lofty Highway 82 is the highest paved road in the United States that crosses the Continental Divide.

From the headwaters, the Roaring Fork River starts collecting water and flows through the towns of Aspen, Woody Creek, Basalt and Carbondale. At each of these towns the Roaring Fork, colloquially called "The Fork," is joined by a creek or river. Highway 82 and the Roaring Fork loosely parallel each other. The river and road intertwine in four places, and at those spots a bridge crosses the Fork. One of the bridges is particularly "dear" to Up-For- Anything-Sam.

～

With just two of us the logistics for the triathlon were simple. The day before the event, we shuttled Sam's car to the confluence; his vehicle would be our ride home after we finished. We left the car at appropriately-named Two Rivers Park, in Glenwood Springs. On our way to Glenwood we dropped off Sam's kayak and boating stuff at my home in Basalt. The morning of the triathlon I planned to pick up Sam, along with his skiing and biking gear.

June 8, before sunrise, Sam and I started our drive to the top of Independence Pass. According to the calendar it was only thirteen days until the summer solstice, the official start of summer, but there was *nothing* summery about the day. On top of the pass at over 12,000 feet, we stepped out of the truck and a biting wind woke me faster than my large mug of strong black coffee. No need for sunglasses, dark heavy clouds were tearing across the sky. Sam and I hustled back into the truck. We were lucky it wasn't a whiteout. The clouds were only spitting graupel, snow which looks like little white Styrofoam® BBs, but sometimes sting one's face like BBs of metal.

Our window of opportunity to complete the Headwaters to Confluence Triathlon (HCT) was small. The road to Independence Pass opened late May, on Memorial Day weekend, after being closed for seven months due to deep snow. And by July 4th, the south-facing mountain would not be ski-able, because too much snow would have melted. We sat in the truck with the engine running and the heater on. Pieces of snow whipped across the parking lot. Thinking I might need to convince him, I said, "Come on Sam, let's give it a go. Remember all the crazy places you've dragged me kayaking?" He was my kayaking coach.

But Up-For-Anything needed no encouragement, "Batman, it's a lovely January-like day in the Rocky Mountains. Let's go skiing!"

While sitting in the tight cab, we finished squirming into our ski clothes. We left the heater blowing to bank as much warmth as possible. Once outside, Sam and I hustled into ski boots, grabbed our packs and started up Blue. Sometimes the mountains are warm and welcoming, and can almost feel smallish. But not today. Blue Mountain had never loomed so large.

An hour later we were halfway up the mountain, and stopped to catch our breath and rest for a few minutes. Graupel continued pelting us. The summit of Blue Mountain was covered in thick dark clouds—it was dumping buckets of snow on top. We pushed upward another ten minutes before Sam stopped.

"Batman, it's a lousy day for the summit. We'd be nuts to go to the top today. Plus we've got a long, long way to go. We need to get out of here." Being somewhat of a purist, I wanted to complete the triathlon from the summit. But my practical side agreed with Sam.

Once we quit grunting our way up Blue, we stopped generating heat. Sam and I turned our backs to the wind and added all our layers of extra clothing. Even facing away from the stiff breeze, the wind acted like a heavy-duty fan and continually blew away our internal heat, chilling us. We removed the climbing skins from the base of our skis and got ready to go. Blue is not especially difficult to ski. So without exerting ourselves very much and getting our blood rapidly circulating, we never warmed up. Skiing down was routine and *cold*.

Back at the truck we started the engine, cranked the heater full blast, and began to thaw out. Getting dressed to bike was as simple as tying one's shoes. Sam and I kept on all our ski clothes, including hat, gloves, and goggles. We changed only our footwear, out of ski boots into biking shoes. The most memorable moment of the first HCT was when we sat on mountain bikes dressed in ski gear and started down the pass.

Cautiously, the two of us crept away from Independence Pass; Highway 82 was dusted with a thin layer of ice and snow. When we hit less slippery pavement, Sam cruised past and hollered, "Time to let 'er rip." It's possible to go scary-fast while cycling down from Independence Pass. We didn't push the pace by pedaling hard, but simply coasted on the curvy road and lightly squeezed the brakes in a couple of tight places, occasionally glancing at the scenery. During the USA Pro Challenge, professional cyclists routinely reach speeds over 55 miles per hour when they bike down from Independence Pass.

All along the eighteen-mile ride and 4,200 vertical-foot descent to Aspen, the air temperature kept rising. Partway down, we switched from ski gloves to biking gloves and from goggles to sunglasses; I left my ski clothes on because it felt good to get a little overheated. With the combination of lower elevation, no wind, and sunny skies, it felt sixty degrees warmer when we got to town. Biking all downhill, without pedaling up, was like receiving a bonus paycheck without doing a lot of hard work.

At Sam's townhouse near Aspen, I turned my daypack upside down and dumped everything out. After munching a quick bite and repacking a few essentials, the two of us were down to shorts and tee-shirts when we biked away from his place.

In Aspen, we left Highway 82 and continued our ride

on the Rio Grande Trail. The eight-foot-wide pedestrian/ bike trail is the former railroad bed for the track that ran between Aspen and Glenwood Springs. Seven miles down the trail, we were rolling past the Woody Creek Tavern when Sam said, "Batman, let's stop at the Tavern and have a quick beer."

"Sounds good to me."

Sam tipped back and emptied his first beer, then asked, "One more?"

"Yeah, sure."

Minutes later, Sam downed his second beer and flashed a mischievous grin. "Another one, Batman?"

This time, I was the one who issued the warning. I used almost the exact words I had heard only hours earlier on Blue Mountain, "We've got a long, long way to go. Sambo, we need to get out of here."

By the time we finished biking from the tavern to my house in Basalt, and then slammed a late lunch while getting dressed to kayak, and then carried our boats to the river, and then... it was 5:00 p.m. before we launched. Our pleasant two-beer buzz was long gone. In June, the sun is high in the sky and the days are the longest of the year. Also in June, the river is high up its banks, at peak flow and moving its fastest, about 5 or 6 mph. But even in fast water, we still had twenty-four miles of river between us and the confluence, and that's a really long distance on the water. Without even calculating the math, I knew we didn't have a ton of time.

I had never kayaked twenty-four miles in a day. Sam had done that many miles only once. I'd hoped for a leisurely float to the confluence; instead we would have to paddle the entire way. The two of us would need every minute of daylight to finish before dark. Both of us wanted to finish the triathlon, but neither of us was looking forward to the possibility of kayaking in the dark.

I'd never kayaked between Basalt and Carbondale, and asked "Sam, what's the river like downstream of Basalt?"

"Umm... let me think. I boated it once, half-zillion years ago. I don't remember much of it."

"Great." I said sarcastically.

He reminded me of why I call him Up-For-Anything-Sam, "Batman, you're right, it is great. You get to kayak a new section of river, and it's in our own backyard. What a bonus!" I muffled my groan. I knew the river between Basalt and Carbondale couldn't be too mean, because it was visited by fly fishermen rowing rafts or dory-style drift boats.

Sam shoved off and I followed. The first confusing thing that happened was the river started braiding, it divided and then divided again. *Which way do we to go?* I wondered. In moments like these it's good to be with a big-boater, someone like Sam who is more experienced. Sam adhered to the standard river rule: when in doubt, follow the channel with the most water.

The next conundrum that surprised us was a number of low-head dams, which are boulders stacked across, or partly across, the river to divert water for irrigation. Upstream of the low-heads it's not always easy to read the river and find the best line over or through the rocks. Especially when the river is screaming-fast and you need to read it quickly, on the fly. Most were no problem but one definitely looked tricky. Scouting was an option—a time-consuming option. Big-boater Sam decided to trust his instincts. One hundred yards above the rock dam, he yelled, "I'm running it. If my line sucks, I'll try to signal you which way to go with my paddle." I didn't say it, but thought to myself, *Great*. His line worked out fine for both of us, despite being blasted in the face by a bunch of cold water, but that's kayaking anyway.

Another bonus, Sam and I started seeing great blue heron—lots of them. The thin birds stand three and a half feet tall on long thin legs. They have an extended S-shaped neck, and a pointed beak which is nearly a foot long and perfectly shaped for spearing or scooping up fish. Everything about heron is long, including their six-foot wingspan. The birds are wary of people and almost always fly away when anyone gets near. But a brave one remained standing at the river's edge, while we silently floated past. It looked a little prehistoric and made me think of a pterodactyl. The imposing bird also made me grateful I was a lot bigger than a trout.

When we reached Carbondale we were halfway to the confluence. The section of river between Basalt and Carbondale had been splashy in spots but had no real rapids, which explains why it's seldom kayaked. The Roaring Fork between Carbondale and Glenwood was a familiar twelve miles. The six miles from Carbondale to the old Black Bridge, the bridge so special to Sam, are rated beginner. And the water between the Black Bridge and the confluence is rated beginner/intermediate, but it might not be so easy for us to navigate in the dark.

Downriver of Carbondale, we saw more heron and stopped paddling to float past a rookery. A few large cottonwood trees had multiple nests, which cradled newborn hatchlings. The day of the triathlon, Sam and I estimated we saw about forty heron total. That was the most either of us had seen in one day.

We rounded a bend in the river and there was the old Black Bridge. The confluence was still six more miles and the sun had already dropped behind a ridge to the west.

"Sam, should I throw you off the Black Bridge again?" I laughed at him.

"I'd like to try one more time. But we don't have enough people to help. Plus it's getting late."

$\sim$

Two years earlier, Up-For-Anything-Sam had guided a group of beginner kayakers— also known as baby-boaters or ducklings—from the Black Bridge to Two Rivers Park in Glenwood. All the kayaks had been carried to the river, except Sam's. One of the ducklings offered to help Sam carry his boat to the water.

"No thanks. I'm going to launch from the bridge." He said casually.

The duckling walked down to the flock of baby-boaters by the water and squawked, "Sam wants to launch from the bridge and needs our help. He can't be serious!"

The covey looked at me because I knew Up-For-Anything best. "I don't think he's kidding."

All six baby-boaters walked back to the Black Bridge. Sure enough, Sam had carried his kayak onto the bridge. Traffic wouldn't be a problem because the Black Bridge had long been retired. Up-For-Anything sat in his boat and stretched his spray-skirt onto the kayak's cockpit. (Kayakers wear a neoprene spray-skirt around the waist, like a skirt, which tightly seals to the kayak and keeps water out.) Sam would have launched himself off the bridge, but he couldn't fit between the black metal guard rails. He needed help with the fifteen-foot drop.

Once in his kayak, with the spray-skirt snugly in place, Sam gave us instructions. "Okay, lift me up and set the boat on top of the guard rail. Don't let go. And don't push me out." He continued to explain and direct, "If I land flat on the water, it'll hurt bad. Let the bow tip down and lift the stern up. I want to vertically pencil into the river." Most of the ducklings thought Sam was crazy.

"Ready Sam?"

"Yeah."

"One, two, three…"

The launch looked perfect. Sam's bow hit first and he completely submerged. But not everything had gone so well; we couldn't see what had happened under the water. When Sam hit the river his spray skirt imploded and popped off his kayak. The boat filled with water and Sam was swamped. Nearly impossible to Eskimo-roll his kayak in that predicament, Up-For-Anything had no choice but to do a "wet-exit" and swim out of his boat.

Seldom do baby-boaters see big-boaters swim. The shocked ducklings, standing on the bridge and far from their kayaks, were unable to help. Three baby-boaters, including me, ran to our boats. The others only gawked as Sam grabbed his kayak and found his paddle. Then, with both hands full, he awkwardly stroked and kicked his way to shore—rescuing himself. Dangerous? No, because the river is relatively mellow downstream of the Black Bridge. Comical? Evidently, because Sam was laughing out loud at himself when he stepped out of the river.

$\sim$

Gratefully, Up-For-Anything-Sam and I arrived at the con-fluence minutes before darkness, during the first HCT. From there we could see the bright lights illuminating the baseball field at Two Rivers Park. They were a welcome sight, but an unnecessary beacon because our eyes had adjusted to the dim light. Relaxed, Sam and I leisurely stroked the last one hundred yards of the triathlon on the Colorado River. The two of rested in our boats for a couple of minutes on the park's concrete boat ramp. Moments later, as we changed into dry clothes and loaded the kayaks, the park lights be-came helpful; the sky had turned completely black.

∼

In the year following the triathlon, I mentioned the event to a few friends and others learned about the adventure by word of mouth. Their usual comments were, "That sounds like a great day. If you ever do it again be sure to let me know. I want to go." That's how the second Headwaters to Confluence Triathlon started with *twenty-five* people.

I pondered... How would the triathlon work out with twenty-five of us? I decided to pencil together a plan—with a relaxed timetable. The day would have to start early, at 6:00 a.m., near City Market in Aspen.

The large size of our group dictated some changes, most significant was the ski. Instead of skiing Blue Mountain, we'd ski 4th of July Bowl. Rather than climb sixteen hundred vertical feet up Blue from Independence Pass, which could take hours with twenty-five of us, we'd hike 60 minutes up a gentle slope to the top of 4th of July Bowl. Plus no one would need specialized mountaineering skis and bindings, everyone could walk in their regular ski boots. Biking would remain the same. Not everybody kayaked, so I planned to ask two boating friends to meet us at the river in Basalt with their rafts.

I penciled in a breakfast stop in Aspen after biking down from Independence Pass. We'd eat in town at a local favorite, the Hickory House. If upscale Aspen had a greasy-spoon, which it doesn't, it would be the Hickory House. Also penciled in was a brief stop at the Woody Creek Tavern for *one* beer or whatever their choice. Lunch would be at my house in Basalt, the Bat House. Unlike the Ironman, this was designed to be a fun adventure and social event, not a grueling race.

The plan was to move together as a loose group at a comfortable pace, with a number of stops along the way to gather everyone together. The brief breaks would also be a chance to rest for a few minutes, look at the scenery and visit. Once on the water it would be easy to stay together. While the triathlon was a long day, I always considered it simply an excellent way to have a great time in the mountains and on the river.

One week before the second HCT, I drove up Highway 82 toward Independence Pass and stopped near the bottom of 4th of July Bowl. It was early morning. In preparation for the upcoming triathlon I wanted to scout for a snow-bridge across the Roaring Fork River. After skiing 4th of July Bowl during the triathlon, everyone would need to cross the river to get back to Highway 82. Often there are snow-bridges, so it's easy to travel over the water. Following a short walk on hard frozen snow, I discovered that the snow-bridges had already melted.

The river looked more like a creek; it was only nine feet wide and about a foot deep. But stepping off the snow bank and walking through icy water would be difficult and miserable for everyone during the triathlon. It's always awkward, extremely slippery, and a bit precarious traipsing in a shallow stream while wearing ski boots. The other unpleasant and time-consuming option, after throwing your skis over the river, would be to send one ski boot flying followed by the second, and then walk through the water barefoot. I've never enjoyed ending a great ski by floundering through a river, with or without ski boots, using ski poles for balance and trying not to fall.

After the quick peek at the river, I motored up to the top of Independence Pass. My plan was to go skiing in an area named Mountain Boy. From the parking lot on the pass I hiked south, uphill, for two miles on a low-angle, broad ridge. The best terrain to ski on Mountain Boy faces east, where the snow gets the first rays of sun and softens early. Once on top of Mountain Boy, I sat on my pack looking east, loving the sunshine on my face and waiting for the snow to change from bulletproof to velvety soft.

While hanging out and waiting for the sun to do its thing, my friend Christi and her ski partner, Betsy, hiked up. I'd never met Betsy. We talked for a few minutes and I mentioned the upcoming event. "Next weekend is the second Headwaters to Confluence Triathlon. It's not a race." I explained the triathlon and invited them. When the time was right, the three of us skied down together. By hiking to the top of Mountain Boy we had earned our turns with energy and sweat. Unhurried, we took our time skiing down.

Each of us savored every turn and being in a natural setting, all without spending a dime on lift tickets. Skiing one at a time, we watched each other carve down perfectly softened, heavenly, corn snow.

Both Christi and Betsy were on very old, lightweight, telemark skis. Some telemark gear is stout and capable of handling any terrain or snow condition, but other "telly" skis are better suited for a mellow Sunday cruise around a snow covered golf course. (Telemark skiers are sometimes called Freeheelers, because only the toe of their boot is attached to the ski.) Old telemark gear works fine on friendly terrain and perfect snow, like we had just skied. But I was concerned after our run. Trying to sound unworried, I said, "If you decide to do the triathlon you may want to bring your heavy-duty alpine skis. The pair you'd use at the ski area. 4th of July Bowl faces north, and without morning sun it will probably be rock-hard. And it's always really steep."

My warning was aimed primarily at Betsy. That morning was first time I had seen her ski, and I knew Betsy would not be happy nor safe with her lightweight skis and boots in 4th of July Bowl. Christi is an excellent skier and comfortable on almost any equipment. She curtly said, "I'll be *fine* on these skis."

Years earlier, I had seen evidence that 4th of July Bowl is a place that can injure. The lower half of the bowl is easy skiing, but the top half includes a steep face. Once while skiing there, I found a broken ski pole and cracked eyeglasses scattered on the snow near the bottom of the steep face. There was also blood dotting the snow. A skier had fallen and taken a slide-for-life. A slide-for-life happens when someone falls on a steep and very firm slope, and they can't self-arrest and stop their fall. Sometimes the fall might be benign and the victim will be shaken but not injured. But other times...

⁓

Spring-skiing in Colorado is different than mid-winter. In springtime, warm days and sunshine soften and "bake" the snowpack, then at night the snow refreezes rock-hard and solid. Skiers want the snow to freeze hard. (This applies to snowboarders also.) If the snow doesn't refreeze solid the skiing will probably be bad. And if the snowpack gets too warm and becomes wet and sloppy, the skiing will definitely be bad and possibly dangerous because of avalanches.

Weather and timing are important considerations for good spring-skiing. Generally, the air temperature drops or rises three degrees for every one thousand vertical feet of change. This is known as the adiabatic lapse rate. The three degrees of change will vary depending on the humidity: dry air will change more than three degrees and moist air will change less than three degrees. A backcountry skier can wake up early at home, look at an outdoor thermometer and do the math. Many who ski near Independence Pass follow a simple guideline: If it's colder than forty degrees early morning in Aspen, it's probably worth getting out of bed.

⁓

Twenty-five of us rendezvoused near City Market in Aspen at 6:00 a.m. on June 5, for the second Headwaters to Confluence Triathlon. Christi showed up but not Betsy, and there were no last minute surprise entrants. I was somewhat relieved, because I knew everyone and their skiing abilities.

The large group caravanned to the top of Independence

Pass. Two people weren't skiing and they planned to move all the vehicles, which carried the bikes, to the bottom of 4th of July Bowl after everyone started. The two also had a more unusual job—bridge building. After shuttling the cars, they unloaded a sturdy metal extension ladder off the roof rack of my truck. Then they carried the ladder to the river and laid it flat over the water, bridging the Roaring Fork. After skiing 4th of July Bowl, each skier would leave their skis on and carefully shuffle across the ladder's metal rungs.

From the parking lot at Independence Pass the triathlon was underway. Excitement filled the rarified air, but the pace was relaxed. The start was not at all like the organized and precisely timed start at the Ironman Triathlon. People in our group began whenever they were ready, either in small groups, pairs, or solo. Up-For-Anything-Sam was among the first skiers to start and guided the way to 4th of July Bowl. I started with the last skiers and stayed in back to lend a hand if needed, but primarily to keep the pace slow so no one felt rushed. The day was like a marathon, or two, and not a sprint. For years I've been saying, *"The slower you go, the more you see."* It was nice to feel relaxed, look at the scenery and gab with friends, while moving slowly enough that no one needed to gasp in the thin air above 12,000 feet.

The weather was cold, but *much* nicer than the first HCT. Another good thing, avalanches would not be a concern because the snow was firm—very firm.

An hour later, we gathered at the top of 4th of July Bowl and got ready to ski. Casually and skiing as a group, we enjoyed a mellow cruise on easy terrain, and then stopped at the break-over above the steep face. While the rest of us were looking down the slope, Rudy was feeling frisky and went first. He ripped high speed, non-stop turns, all the way to the bottom of the face. A second skier followed when Rudy neared the end of the steep pitch. I went third. My plan was to go partway down and stop. I deliberately displayed a very different technique than Rudy's and cautiously cranked conservative turns on the hard frozen slope. My turns were loud, and the vibration from chattering skis on boiler-plate snow felt like it rattled the fillings in my teeth.

About one-quarter of the way down, I slowed to a stop and moved out of the main ski line to wait and watch. Standing on the face provided a stark reminder of just how steep the place was. Intuitively, everyone skied one at a time. When ready, each skier took their turn, skied past me and continued down to join the growing group at the bottom of the face. Christi was the ninth or tenth skier. She was on her lightweight telemark skis. Her first, second and third turns went well.

Damn! Christi bobbled on her fourth turn and fell on her fifth. Instantly she began accelerating, sliding out of control, un-helmeted, toward the rocks and trees below. She had no hope of stopping herself. If Christi were lucky her hospital stay would be short.

Sam screamed, "Batman, get in front of her!" I thought, *No way.* Because after she slams into me, we are both going to the morgue.

When Christi got close to me I started to ski. She had already slid 150 yards. Fortunately I could ski as fast as she was falling. I controlled my descent so I was skiing next to her. At times we were only a few feet apart. Christi was falling in a straight line and my ski tracks were like a series of S's in a vertical line. I skied toward Christi and when I got right next to her, I turned away. Then I quickly turned back toward Christi so I could watch her. Toward her and away, toward her and away... She was silently sliding on her side, with her feet below her head. I was skiing next to her and just a little downhill. Now what?

For a millisecond, Christi slowed a tiny bit when she hit a little bump. An opening. A chance. I skied beneath her. Instantly she hit my legs and knocked me over. I landed on top of her. The two of us were now tangled together and sliding. Somehow I managed to keep one ski in control, swiftly placed it on the snow, and we skidded to a stop.

No high-fives or fist-bumps. No hoots or hollers. Christi was trembling. I felt like throwing up. We lay on the snow getting our bearings. Each of us was also going through a mental checklist for injuries.

When I looked around, there was Sam. What a welcome surprise. He had chased us down the face, and when we stopped moving he'd caught up to us. Standing only a few feet downhill from Christi and me, Sam had positioned himself as a guardian, in case we started sliding again.

"Are you two okay?" he asked. We were, but each of us only nodded.

Of the remaining skiers at the top of the face, no one ripped down like Rudy had done earlier. Each skier cautiously descended, not wanting to become another "car wreck." Concerned, every skier glanced at us on their way past; some of their eyes lingered longer. They were different than rubberneckers at a car wreck. We were all friends and any of them would have stopped if we had gestured for help.

I untangled myself from Christi and stood up. She sat up and moved her skis to a better position, to keep from sliding. After a few minutes, the jitters in her legs subsided and Christi tentatively stood on her skis. She was still wobbly on her feet. But it was more comfortable, and safer, for her to be standing on her skis rather than lying on the snow. I gently placed my hand on her shoulder, "I'm glad you're okay." After an incident like that, it's nice to be reminded that one is okay.

A little small talk between Sam, Christi and me helped establish some normalcy. Christi didn't say much. Several minutes passed, and when it appeared her pulse had dropped back to normal, I asked, "Christi, what do you think? Are you ready to move?"

"Let's get out of here," she answered. Sam was downhill from us and the least shook-up, so he went first. None of us started turning right away, but cautiously side-slipped on our skis. Then Sam hopped a turn, which helped our confidence and got us skiing. The three of us tentatively turned our way down the last of the steep pitch and joined our friends.

In mortuary silence, the group stood around looking up at the face and at each other. The excitement in the air had been replaced by subdued quiet. Intentionally, using an extremely silly voice, Stuart broke the tension, "That *certainly* was exciting." Stuart made everyone laugh, or at least smile. With each of us breathing easier, Rudy once again led the way down the gentler terrain to the makeshift bridge.

Sam, Christi and I, in that order, were the last to go. Christi fell twice on the easy terrain. The first time she slid into a small tree but was okay. On her second tumble she stopped where she tipped over. Her mind was seriously shaken and her legs were still wobbly. Christi and I stuck together like a big brother and little sister until we reached the ladder.

Once Christi was safely across the "bridge" Sam spoke to me without a smile, "Batman, does your nickname still feel odd?"

His question was wordlessly answered with shrugged shoulders, rolled eyes, and a facial expression that said Oh-my-God.

Skiing across the extension ladder was easier than it may sound. Having skis on made shuffling over the metal ladder rungs more stable than without them. Using the improvised bridge was an entertaining first for everyone.

The bike ride, breakfast, and sitting still while eating all helped settle Christi's nerves. A slide-for-life is a mind altering experience. I know this firsthand. Fortunately, my one harrowing misadventure was physically harmless and not too lengthy. But mentally— no one ever forgets. Most minds are tweaked and steep ski runs look much more intimidating. Nevertheless, following breakfast, Christi was somewhat back to her old self and wanted to continue.

From the Hickory House, the group's next stop was the locally notorious Woody Creek Tavern. Twenty-five of us swamped the bartender and briefly imbibed. I can't be certain, but I'm pretty sure Up-For-Anything-Sam was the last one out the door. Then we cycled ten more miles to Basalt and ate lunch at the Bat House. (An architect/friend named the house when she drafted the building plans.) After dressing in river attire, everyone walked to the water to meet Michael and Gregg with their rafts.

Rather than two people and two rafts, we found four rafts and twelve people. "Batman, I decided to invite a few friends to the floating party," Michael howled from the stern of his boat. I couldn't believe it—we now had thirty-seven people. I started kayaking with the odd feeling that something was missing. Somehow we only had thirty-six life jackets and I'd given mine to a rafter whose face I didn't recognize. I wasn't too worried, if I accidentally swam there would be *plenty* of help.

Stuart, who had delivered the perfect line at the base of the steep face in 4th of July Bowl, is a determined and gutsy guy. He wanted to kayak. Stuie hadn't kayaked in eleven years and even back then he hadn't boated that much. But knowing that he was comfortable on the water and wasn't likely to freak if something went wrong, we outfitted him in some old gear.

In the first couple of miles, Stuart tipped over and couldn't Eskimo-roll his boat, so he had to swim. This happened not once—but twice. Both swims stopped the flotilla while we gathered kayak, paddle, and Stuie. Then we burned more daylight helping him drain his boat and letting Stuie catch his breath and rebalance his brain. More time ticked away while we helped him squeeze back into his kayak and launch. I hated to say it to my good friend Stuart, but after his second swim I told him, "Sorry mate, but keep in mind, three strikes and you're out. Out of the kayak that is, and onto a raft. We need to get to Glenwood before dark and we've got a long way to go." Stuart's two swims must have washed off eleven years of rust, because he kayaked the rest of the way without incident.

Tired but elated, and with no further mishaps, thirty-seven of us arrived at the junction of the Roaring Fork and Colorado Rivers. Because of vividly contrasting colors, confluence lines can sometimes be beautiful, intriguing, and mesmerizing. Other times the merging rivers look identical. That day the confluence line was a distinctive red and green; the Colorado was muddy red and the Roaring Fork was clear-green. The group floated a short distance on the Colorado and beached at the concrete boat ramp in Two Rivers Park; it was after sunset, but thankfully before dark.

All the bikes were at the Bat House, so we met there for an impromptu dinner and celebration. Everyone who started the second HCT finished. Between a penciled in schedule, logistics, and shuttles; an extension ladder, gear, and more gear; sips, swims, and a memorable slide; this and that—the second Headwaters to Confluence Triathlon had all worked out.

~

The third HCT had no schedule and no large group, just an early start with a close friend, Steve-O-Remo. Despite the lack of a timetable, the day went like clockwork. On a gorgeous, classic Colorado, blue-bird-sunny-day, we summited Blue Mountain. Spectacular. We biked past the Woody Creek Tavern—without stopping. Our only minor glitch came just down-road from the tavern. Steve-O and I heard a familiar sound, hissing air. Before the unwelcome sound ended, speedy Steve-O said, "Batman, let me fix that flat tire for you." He had been a mountain-bike guide for ten years, and for him to fix a flat was like washing grubby dishes, not fun but not a problem. The rest of the ride to Basalt was smooth and easy.

I don't remember what time we launched, but darkness would not be an issue. Before we got on the river Steve-O said, "Batman, I've never kayaked from Basalt to Carbondale and haven't been in my boat in two years."

"Don't worry. You'll be fine. I know the line down the river, and you've kayaked water much rougher than this." The low-head dams were no big deal; I found the best way over the rocks. We floated past a bald eagle perched at the apex of a tall, riverside, ponderosa pine. The lone raptor and the two kayakers stared at each other. We also saw lots of great blue heron, but not forty like the first HCT. With hours to spare, Steve-O and I floated into sunny Two Rivers Park. The cliché, *the third time is the charm*, was true for the third HCT. For the first time, the triathlon had been completed from the summit of Blue Mountain. The purist in me was content.

$$\sim$$

HCT number four was simple and a bit lonely, I went solo. The triathlon had been in the back of my mind for weeks and I had been looking for a window of opportunity. The window was opening the next day. I had the day off from work, and both the snow on Blue Mountain and the weather would be perfect.

The day before the triathlon, in late afternoon, I packed my gear and drove to the top of Independence Pass. An early start the next morning would be easy, because I spent a comfortable night in the back of my truck. Getting home from the confluence would be equally easy. I was now living in Glenwood Springs and my wife had helped me leave a car at Two Rivers Park.

The morning of the triathlon, I dropped the truck's tailgate and crawled out of bed. While getting dressed and packing, I gulped down two cups of cold instant coffee. (My addiction is to caffeine, not flavor.) Feeling well rested, I headed up Blue for what was a relatively painless climb to the summit.

On top of the peak I peeled off damp undergarments and bundled up in lots of warm clothes. Because of the early start, I had time to relax on the summit. With binoculars I gazed full circle, 360 degrees, and looked at nine of Colorado's fifty-four 14,000 foot mountains. I also enjoyed the view of countless lower peaks, including Sunlight Peak, the tallest mountain near Glenwood Springs. My binoculars fixated on that peak, because it was fifty-plus miles away, and a strong reminder of how far I had left to go. An hour later it was time to get moving; if the confluence hadn't been the final destination it would have been easy to stay even longer.

Some people wonder how anyone can spend hours on top of a mountain. To them I say, "Think about lying on an idyllic beach, or being in a museum with incredible art. What's the hurry?"

Rather than bike down from Independence Pass, I started the truck, rolled down both windows, shifted into neutral, and coasted to Aspen. I wanted to feel cold wind blowing on my face, like biking, but without the hassle of hitchhiking back to Independence Pass the next day to get my truck. Not exactly like riding a bike, but the practical side of me was happy. The rest of the triathlon was simple and glorious, but yes, a tiny bit lonely.

The fifth Roaring Fork Headwaters to Confluence Triathlon has yet to happen. It'll be great to do it again—but next time with at least one friend and fewer than thirty-six.

Extra Bits

Monkey see, monkey do... I learned a great deal about kayaking from Up-For-Anything-Sam— not all of which was prudent. One day a group of kayakers were putting in at the old Black Bridge. I was the big-boater, coach for a gaggle of ducklings, about a half-dozen baby-boaters. I remembered the time I saw Sam launch off the Black Bridge and thought, *that could be fun.*

We started the same drill that we had done with Up-For-Anything many years earlier. I sat in my boat and pulled the spray skirt on. The baby-boaters lifted my kayak and set me on the Black Bridge's metal guard rail. "Ready, Mark?" I nodded.

"One, two..." Just before three, Andy, the most experienced of the baby-boaters, started screaming, "No, no, no! Don't throw him, don't throw him!" Just then, a raft full of people floated under the Black Bridge. Immediately their heads snapped around to look at the crazy guy in a kayak about to be thrown off the bridge. Like merging onto a highway when driving, Andy had wisely looked upstream just before the countdown hit three. After the raft floated downstream, the launch and landing went fine, but Oh-my-God I'd come within half-a-breath of recklessly crashing onto a raft full of people.

Blue Mountain.

Independence Pass, day of first triathlon.

Sam and author on top of Independence Pass.

Doug Nehasil and Dave Lofland skiing Fourth of July Bowl, *not* during triathlon. Photo by Lee Miller.

Sam in front of Bat House, prior to kayaking to Glenwood Springs.

Black Bridge at very low water, photo taken looking downstream. Photo by Cindy Rogers

A Little Geology and Geography

An Acre?

Making a Molehill
Out of a Mountain

An Acre?

How big is an acre of land? What does an acre look like?

From an early age, I always wondered how big is an acre of land? When my parents bought a brand new house in the suburbs of San Francisco, my Mom proudly informed me and my sisters, "Our new house sits on a large lot; it's a quarter of an acre." The new home was the first place Mom had ever lived where a mortgage payment, rather than rent, was due at the first of each month. Our parcel of land was oddly shaped and sloped in different directions. To me, a six-year-old, a quarter of an acre looked confusing.

There are 640 acres in a section of land, which is one square mile (one mile by one mile). And there are 43,560 square feet in an acre. Is this helping? Can you picture it? I don't think so. Neither can I.

My first real estate purchase was 3.13 acres of raw land. It was another odd-shaped parcel. Plus the lot sloped steeply and even included a red sandstone cliff.

I was still confused. What would a nice, flat, and rectangular shaped acre of land look like?

∽

During a real estate class, I was reminded that there are 640 acres in a square mile and 43,560 square feet in an acre. In class my mind started to daydream and wander, and a *football field* came to mind. Maybe I could compare an acre of land to a football field. Almost every high school has one. We know how big a football field is. We know what it looks like.

In class I started to play with my calculator.

A football field is 50 yards by 100 yards, or 150 feet by 300 feet. (That is without the small end-zone at each end of the field.)

Simple math: Multiply 150 feet by 300 feet.

150 x 300 equals 45,000. A football field is 45,000 square feet.

An acre (43,560 square feet) is basically the size of a football field.

Mystery solved.

Making a Molehill
Out of a Mountain

It's hard for me to imagine gigantic mountains vanishing. But it happened. And it's still happening. About 230-250 million years ago the Ancestral Rocky Mountains was an ancient mountain range that dominated the landscape of what would later become Colorado—but it no longer exists. The peaks were eroded to a flat, rolling terrain.

The formidable Rocky Mountains of today run from Canada to New Mexico. They include the Continental Divide, the tall spine of North America which drains surface water east to the Atlantic Ocean, west to the Pacific, or north to the Arctic Ocean. Marveling at rock-solid mountains in Colorado, or anywhere, it's difficult to envision them going away.

The many forces of erosion are powerful, they include: wind, ice, rain, hail, melting snow, ocean waves, glaciers, earthquakes, and gravity. Water, especially in the form of running water, which ranges from rivulets to raging rivers, is among the strongest forces eroding the Earth's surface. The immense Grand Canyon was carved by the Colorado River, and the river continues to dig deeper into the Earth. Rainwater and other force of erosion continue to widen the canyon.

We know the Earth is old, about 4.6 billion years old. So the forces of erosion could have taken a long, long time to have "eaten" the Ancestral Rocky Mountains, or any mountain range. But how long?

When I read James Michener's book, *Centennial*, I began to better understand how long it could take for a solid mountain to be razed flat. The second chapter, titled *The Land* contains a telling paragraph.

Paraphrasing from Michener:* To understand how a 10,000 foot mountain disappears in forty million years, it's important to think about time. What has happened? In one million years the mountain has lost two hundred and fifty feet. Over a thousand year period the mountain has lost only three inches. The loss per year would be imperceptible to the human eye.

After reading this, I figured out that the amount of erosion Michener was describing would have been 3/1000 of an inch in one year, the thickness of a sheet of paper. If a 10,000-foot mountain is eroded the thickness of a sheet of paper—every year, for 40 million years—it makes the mountain vanish.

In the Earth's life, how long is 40 million years? I thought about comparing the Earth to a ninety-year-old man or woman, and started doing a little math. I figured out that if the 4.6 billion year old Earth was a 90-year-old person, 40 million years of its life would be about nine months of the 90-year-olds life. Nine months... not much time in a long life.

Critters

Would I? Would You?

One Tragedy and Two Saves

Would I? Would You?

My good friend Steve was on an early morning run. The sun had just begun to lighten the night sky; it was crisp and cold in the Centennial State, Colorado. In the distance, down a quiet two-lane road, Steve saw a mound of something on the side of the pavement. He had recently seen a herd of deer in his yard and thought perhaps it was a road-killed deer. But as he got closer, Steve could see that the mound was a person.

The man lying crumpled on the edge of the pavement was another runner. Steve recognized him. He was a local legend, seventy-year-old Paul Driskill, and he was in terrible shape. Barely conscious, Paul was uncontrollably shivering, gasping for air and struggling to breathe. Paul was easily recognizable because of his scraggly gray beard and distinctive running clothes. He often wore the same pair of shorts, which were cut very short and resembled the United States flag. In addition, Paul was known for not wearing gloves to keep his hands warm, but using a pair of rag-wool socks.

Paul was legendary, not because of his speed, but because of his love of running and his determination. Paul had achieved a long, long streak of consecutive days running. Daily, he had run thirteen miles—a half-marathon—for fourteen straight years. Weather be damned, he ran every day. But if the conditions outside were really rough, he ran his miles in the gymnasium of the elementary school where he had been a teacher.

Steve did what most of us would have done in that situation; he called 911 and did his best to keep Paul warm. Steve also carried on a gentle-voiced, one-way conversation to reassure Paul while they waited for help. When the police and ambulance arrived Steve assisted them, and then answered many questions that day and over the following days.

When Steve found Paul he wasn't sure what had happened to him. Paul's eyes were open but he never spoke a word. Steve thought Paul might have had a heart attack, or tripped and taken a bad fall. After the ambulance raced away, the officers on the scene began to investigate. They discovered fresh skid marks on the pavement. Most telling, the officers had noticed that Paul was wearing only one shoe. Sometimes when a pedestrian is struck hard by a vehicle they are knocked out of their shoes. The police surmised that Paul had been the victim of a hit-and-run accident.

Two months later, Steve was on another morning run. But this time, I'm not sure how many of us would have acted as heroically as Steve.

Steve saw a cat-sized animal stumbling down the road. Sensing death, five or six ravens were flying four feet above the animal. As he got closer, Steve realized the animal had its head stuck inside of a Yoplait® yogurt container. Yoplait's uniquely shaped containers have a smaller top than bottom. And what unfortunate animal was in this awful predicament? A skunk.

Steve watched for several minutes. From the looks of things it seemed like the critter had been in this mess for a long time. The skunk was blindly blundering around and appeared exhausted.

Once again Steve called the police. This time he was connected to the Department of Wildlife. From his conversation with the DOW, Steve realized they might be of little help. And he now feared that if the DOW showed up their solution might be to put the lowly animal out of its misery, euthanize. If Steve wanted to help, he was going to have take matters into his own hands—literally.

Lucky for Steve the morning was cold, so he was wearing gloves. Steve had time to think. First, out loud, he said to himself, "Wish me luck." Then he walked up to the skunk and said, "I'm here to help you little fella. I'm going to take it off your head. Then I'm getting out of here, and you're getting out of here, and everything's going to be okay."

Steve thought removing the yogurt container would be quick and easy. Not so. When he reached down and pulled, the container didn't budge. Steve pulled harder, and when he did he lifted the skunk a few feet off the ground. One would think that gravity would help to remove the container. But no, the skunk was still stuck.

Steve had already done much more than many of us would have. And he was willing to do more. Steve started to shake the container up and down. He also moved his other hand next to the skunk. Steve was getting ready to do what few of us would—grab the animal that few people love—and pull.

Fortunately, Steve's active shaking worked and the skunk's head popped out. The skunk fell to the ground and the two looked at each other. The skunk seemed dazed but quickly recovered. No sounds or words were exchanged.

Luckily for Steve nothing was exchanged.

The smelly black critter with white stripes scurried away and never lifted its tail to spray. Steve hurried off in the opposite direction. He then used his cell phone a second time to call the DOW. Steve simply stated, "Hello Department of Wildlife, the skunk incident has been resolved."

Extra Bits

Yoplait has recognized that their yogurt containers are a problem for wildlife. Steve's skunk incident was not the first time this had happened. Yoplait has added a small plastic rim at the base of their yogurt containers, so an animal can get a grip with its claws. Yoplait has also added a warning, "Protect Wildlife Crush Cup Before Disposal."

Paul Driskill sustained a myriad of serious injuries when he was struck by the car. After an ambulance arrived, he was transported to the local hospital and later airlifted to a large trauma center. During his emergency care, Paul's heart stopped and he needed resuscitation. Many people helped save Paul's life. Without a doubt, Paul was very lucky Steve found him and acted quickly, or Paul probably would have died on the side of the road.

Two months after the accident Paul participated in an organized five-kilometer walk/run. He was steadied by the use of a cane and the arm of his granddaughter. Paul Driskill passed away three years after he was hit by the vehicle. The big-hearted man and Jeannie, his wife of fifty years, had helped many people. In his obituary Paul was described as a "Champion of the Downtrodden."

(The total miles run by Paul during his streak: Days in one year 365, multiplied by 13 miles per day, multiplied by 14 years. 365 x 13 x 14 = 66,430 miles. The Earth's circumference is about 25,000 miles)

One Tragedy and Two Saves

"Everybody can be great... because anybody can serve. You don't have to have a college degree to serve. You don't have to make your subject and verb agree to serve. You only need a heart full of grace. A soul generated by love."

Martin Luther King Jr.

Stotting is the term for the unique way mule deer spring off all four legs at once. Then they gracefully glide through the air. Sometimes their legs remain straight, like four pogo-sticks in unison. Other times their legs are bent at the knee, with the lower part of each limb parallel to the ground. Once in the air they seem to float. Deer are capable of leaping over the tallest humans and can bound a distance of over twenty feet. Almost all animals are nimble on their hooves, paws, pads, or feet and move athletically. But deer are a special joy to watch because they stot.

Some pictures in our minds are indelibly imprinted, and like ink—they can't be erased. One of the saddest images in my brain is of a dead deer draped over a barbed wire fence. I didn't see it happen, but something went terribly wrong when the unfortunate animal attempted to jump over the fence. Maybe the deer tripped, or got its legs tangled in the barbed wire, or perhaps it never saw the fence. But for some reason, the animal didn't clear the obstacle and its upper abdomen landed on the top strand of wire. Unable to free itself, it died.

I wish I had found the deer while it was alive. Maybe I could have cut the wire and helped. Or when all hope was gone—heartbreakingly pulled the trigger—because sometimes the most humane choice is a bullet.

I'm not a hunter or a gun-guy. At times I've shot handguns and rifles, but I own neither. I've never intentionally killed anything larger than a pack rat. I set traps because the opportunistic critters had moved into a dilapidated garage I was renting and they were making a huge mess. Occasionally I've taken the life of a large fish, which provided several delicious meals. Yet, if I had found the deer while it was alive, but injured beyond hope, I would have borrowed a firearm or called a hunter friend to finish what the barbed wire had started.

The dead deer hung folded over the top strand of barbed wire for several days before someone removed the animal. The fence line was on a remote ranch near where I was living. Most likely the rancher or the Department of Wildlife removed the deer. For years I drove past the tragic spot, and almost every time the image appeared in my mind.

My friend John once told me about the time he found a large owl hanging upside down, tangled and trapped, in a barbed wire fence. The owl was alive. My guess is the bird was hunting, flying low and looking for prey. Or maybe its eyes were already focused on its next meal. For some reason, the owl never saw the fence.

John, who has since passed away, walked slowly towards the bird. In his hand was a Swiss Army knife. The owl's head was not completely trapped by the wire and the bird watched as John approached. When John got closer he began to hum and speak softly. Then he knelt down by the big-eyed bird of prey. John was aware that its sharp talons and beak could inflict painful injury to soft human skin, especially his face. When John told me the story, he said, "I felt like the owl knew I was there to help."

He opened his Swiss Army knife, not to the knife blades but the scissors. To me, the scissors on the distinctive red knife always seemed more like a toy than a tool. But with those tiny scissors John began cutting feathers. His feeling about the owl was confirmed, because the raptor never struggled, panicked, or struck at him.

John kept snipping away until the bird fell to the ground. Once freed, the owl fully surveyed the scene as only an owl is capable of doing. First, it rotated its head 180 degrees and glanced behind. Then it turned almost 360 degrees in the opposite direction. Lastly it straightened its head to look forward. A few seconds later, just before it flew away, the owl looked at John one last time with its huge luminous eyes.

Prior to moving on, John picked up one of the feathers he'd cut to keep as a reminder of his good fortune to have been eye-to-eye with a long eared owl.

～

Judy, an older buddy, and I were hiking on a dirt trail next to a small mountain stream. The clear, cold, fast-moving water was home to rainbow and brown trout. We saw a small amount of litter associated with fishing—old bait containers on the ground and some fishing line snarled in the stream-side vegetation.

Walking farther up the trail, we noticed a gray bird moving unnaturally in a small tree by the water. When Judy and I got closer, it began to wildly flap its wings. The bird was terrified of us but it didn't fly away—it couldn't. Once exhausted, it stopped moving and seemed suspended in mid-air. The winged creature was a gray jay, and it was hanging from the end of a fishing line that was tangled in the tree's branches. In the side of the jay's beak was a bright, barbed fishing hook, a lure.

An ineffective fisherman must have miscast his line and landed it in the tree. The discarded line and lure remained in the tree, where the shiny object caught the attention of the jay. When the bird struck at the barbed hook, instead of an anticipated mouthful of food, it got a beak full of sharp metal.

We couldn't reach the bird from the ground. To help, one of us would have to risk a short climb up the thin tree. The tree was not growing straight, but at an angle towards the creek. Below the tree, the ground dropped off and was covered with jagged boulders. I headed up the tree, wishing I really was Batman, or perhaps some character known as Monkey Man, because a fall would hurt.

As I gingerly shimmied up the skinny tree, my ears were tuned for the sounds of cracking wood. Judy asked, "Can I help?"

"Yeah, brace the tree." So she wedged her back into the angled trunk to help support the tree. Trying to be weightless, I climbed slowly, hoping not to come crashing down on Judy or the boulders. The bird was going crazy in a frantic fit of panic. Once exhausted, it hung motionless. After a very brief rest the jay started flapping madly, again trying to escape.

Reaching for the fishing line, I grabbed it four feet above the bird. Then I pulled and easily snapped the thin line, breaking it free from the branch. With one hand gripping the line and the other holding onto the tree, I started down. The gray jay looked like a fish on the end of the line, as it flopped and flailed in the air desperately trying to get away.

I moved a short distance down the tree, bringing the frightened being within Judy's reach. When the bird was spent and stopped moving, she captured it in her hands. With Judy cradling the bird, I let go of the line and hustled out of the tree. She continued holding the small feathered critter while I carefully removed the barbed hook from its beak. Judy set the jay on the ground and with the speed of a spark it flew to a safe perch, high in a nearby tree.

Barbed wire and barbed hooks—a barb to wildlife.

Hard to Believe

Leonid Meteor Showers

In the Presence of Eagles

Leonid Meteor Showers

November 18, 2001. The front page of the day's newspaper should have read:

SPECTACULAR LEONID METEOR SHOWER
TONIGHT!!!
Set Your Alarm Clock!
Do Not Miss It! Get Your Butt Out Of Bed!

Alas, the paper had the usual headlines about misdeeds and mayhem. But somewhere deep in the folds of newsprint I spotted a small headline about a meteor shower. I almost needed a magnifying glass to read the story in tiny print.

From the article, I learned the Leonid meteor shower was an annual event. Every year there are many named meteor showers, and the Leonid got its name because it appears to originate from the constellation Leo. I also discovered that most meteor showers occur when Earth passes through a stream of icy dusty debris shed by comets. Some years the Leonid is less spectacular, because the Earth scarcely touches the stream of debris. The best view of the Leonid depends on where you live on the planet, primarily which hemisphere, north or south. The Leonid meteor shower is difficult to predict— but not the one that was going to happen tonight in 2001.

The most compelling part of the article: This year during the peak hours, midnight to sunrise, it would be possible to see between 300 and 500 shooting stars an hour. Three hundred to five hundred shooting stars in an hour... That seemed unbelievable.

I thought many years back, to a college astronomy class. The teacher told us on a normal night a shooting star would occur about once every ten minutes. That would be six in an hour. If you were looking in the wrong direction, you could wait a long time before you saw even one.

The professor also told us that most meteors are the size of a grain of sand or a tiny pebble. A grain of sand? That fact still seems impossible. When the tiny particle hits our upper atmosphere, 30 to 80 miles above the surface, moving at thousands of miles per hour, the friction between the two creates searing heat which ignites the particle. If the meteor survives its flight and lands on Earth it is called a meteorite.

I didn't set my alarm. For me to sleep through the night is as rare as a solar eclipse. Before falling asleep, I did the math. Three hundred to five hundred shooting stars in an hour would be one every seven to twelve seconds. I was skeptical. I'd have to see it to believe.

On the night of the Leonid, my girlfriend Jen and I were sleeping in a small travel trailer, which was parked on a couple hundred acre parcel of ranchland that she owned. The land is many miles from the nearest town and city lights. In the thin air at 7500 feet in elevation and away from the glow of any lights, star-gazing on her property had always been good.

As usual I woke in the middle of the night, that night around 1:00 a.m. In my foggy haze between sleep and awareness, I saw a lengthy and bright shooting star out the window. There was a second one, and then another lit up the sky. "Jen, wake up. It looks like the meteor shower is happening."

We threw on some clothes and stepped outside. The shower of lights was more than just happening. It was an astounding array like nothing either of us had ever seen. Fire-in-the-sky was everywhere. Single streaks arced great distances across the sky, and clusters of falling stars were mind-blowing. Some of the shooting stars were bright enough to cast shadows. There were only momentary pauses in the action. My jaw didn't drop, but it could have.

The two of us went back into the trailer, not to return to bed, but to put on more clothes. We were going to be outside in the chilly mountain air for a long time.

On a far corner of Jen's land was another travel trailer, where her twenty-two-year-old son, Glen, lived. "We should wake up Glen," I suggested.

Jen is an extremely enthusiastic and brave woman. I assumed she'd say, "Great idea. I'll get him up." But instead she said, "There is no way I'm going into the lair of the bear, much less disrupt his slumber. *You* can wake Glen out of hibernation."

Taken aback, I said, "Let's slowly stroll to Glen's place. If I count fifty meteors before we get to his front door, I'm knocking on it." Leisurely, Jen and I walked on the long dirt driveway between the two metal homes. But mostly we stood still and gawked. When I started counting shooting stars, I also looked at my watch. I quit counting—twenty minutes later—when I'd seen a hundred.

Glen wasn't exactly a redneck and I wasn't exactly a hippie, but we didn't exactly see things the same way. We'd had our rough patches. Glen liked some rock and roll, but without the raunchy. And I enjoyed some country music, but without the twangy voice and soap-opera lyrics. We both liked the outdoors, Glen looking through the scope of a rifle and me through the lens of a camera. Both of us loved Jen, but neither of us liked it when the other bickered with her. Where politics was concerned, we knew better than to even get started. Snow skiing was our best bond.

Glen didn't sleep with a loaded 44 magnum handgun under his pillow, but he was well-armed. His trailer was larger than Jen's and had one bedroom. He slept with the bedroom door closed. When we got to Glen's front door, Jen put her lips to my ear and teasingly whispered, "Batman, I hope your shotgun-shield is up and working." I didn't knock. With the stealth of a ghost, I turned the unlocked doorknob. Hoping the front door wouldn't creak, I inched it open just a crack.

"Glen, wake up, it's Mark." I said softly. A little louder, I repeated myself, "Glen, wake up, it's Mark." Little by little, I raised my voice and repeated myself.

Eventually, I heard a groggy, "I'm awake. I heard you the first time. What's up?"

"Glen everything is fine, there's no problem. But you've got to see this meteor shower."

"Okay, I'm getting up. It better be good."

After half an hour of star gazing, Glen declared, "Mark, I never thought I would be saying this to you. But thanks for waking me."

Things between us were looking up.

An earlier Leonid meteor shower, in 1998, had made an impression on two professional astronomers. This is an excerpt from the NASA Headline News, dated November 8, 2001.* It was written by one of the astronomers in anticipation of the Leonid of 2001, which would so amaze Jen and me. Below is how he described the Leonid Meteor Shower he saw in 1998, and what he speculated about 2001:

I'll never forget the night of November 17, 1998. It was cold outside my mountain home at 9000 feet. The skies were crystal clear. And it was very dark.

That is, except for the fireballs.

I was sky watching with a friend, both of us experienced astronomers. Nevertheless, we stared upwards like novices, slack-jawed, as if we had never seen the sky before.

We were witnessing the annual Leonid meteor shower. But these were no ordinary Leonids. They were bright, vivid, shadow-casting fireballs. Every five minutes or so we saw one as bright as Venus, and a fair number would have outshined a Full Moon. Some of the most startling, left behind glowing trails of debris that lingered in the sky, twisting and turning as they were sheared by high-altitude winds.

It was unforgettable.

*Google search of "Leonid meteor shower 2001" led to http://science.nasa.gov/science-news/science-at-nasa/2001/ast08nov_1/

In years since I've heard sky watchers refer to that event as the "1998 Leonid fireball storm." But it wasn't really a storm at all. Meteor rates that night never exceeded a few hundred shooting stars per hour. We define a meteor storm to be times when observers can see 1000 or more per hour. The Leonids of 1998—as spectacular as they were—were not a full-fledged storm.

But the Leonids of 2001 will be.

What's coming on November 18, 2001 could be the biggest event since 1966, when North Americans enjoyed a Leonid storm numbering 100,000 shooting stars per hour.

In the Presence of Eagles

The first story in *Bat Tales* is "Eagles on the Highway." For many personal reasons, it's the most special to me. Finding two electrocuted golden eagles was a terribly sad—yet an amazing—experience. It was a rare event and I never expected there would be a sequel. This story is a sequel.

Dan is a dear friend. In the past three decades I've seldom called him Dan; he's better known as "Hangtime." Early one evening on the fourth Thursday of November, Thanksgiving Day, Hangtime left his home on the Front Range, near Denver. Before hitting the highway he cleaned the last morsel of pumpkin pie off his plate, kissed his wife and two kids, and affectionately hugged the sweetest mother-in-law in the world. Then with a swollen belly, he hopped in his car and headed west.

Early the following day I left my home in the mountains of western Colorado, and watched the sunrise in my rearview mirror. The two of us planned to rendezvous in Utah at one of our favorite patches of desert and camp for a few days.

At home in Colorado, Hangtime and I each have a full gamut of adult responsibilities—jobs, bills, mortgages, doctor visits, family obligations, and... But when we get together in the desert we are like two big kids. We play hard. At times our laughter is painful, and sometimes sounds like two 350-pound hogs snorting at one another. We also have heart-to-heart talks. After catching up on the latest news about each other's family, our conversation shifts. The questions are personal and pertinent, the discussion soulful and spiritual. We're not blood, but we're brothers.

On our desert trips together, we often have one or two children with us and sometimes up to four kids. But this time it was just the two of us. I don't know why, but when we're together we only use our nicknames.

Lifelong nicknames often materialize out of nowhere. It strikes me as ironic that something as permanent as a name can happen so haphazardly. Hangtime and I first met at the sand volleyball courts in Aspen and started playing doubles together. A few years later, he and I were playing in a volleyball tournament and his timing was off. Ever the competitor, when Hangtime went to the net to pound the ball at the opposition, he was anxious and jumping early. Because he was jumping too soon, he needed to hang in the air and wait for the ball to come down before spiking it. He seemed to defy gravity and hung in the air forever. After several mistimed leaps, which he miraculously hit for winners, I started saying, "Nice shot, Hangtime. Way to go, Hangtime. Hangtime, great..." The name stuck.

∿

Around 11:00 a.m. on Friday, I found Hangtime at our camp. Both of us were ready for a walk and he asked, "Batman, want something to eat before we go hiking?"

"I'm still stuffed from dinner last night. I'm feeling like a bloated collared lizard who just choked down a big fat grasshopper. I can hardly move."

"I'm pretty full myself," he agreed. "Let's just go for a

hike."

As we strolled, I said, "Thanksgiving has become my favorite holiday. When I was a young kid, Christmas and my birthday were the best. Next was Halloween. Gifts and candy were hard to top. The last day of the school year was also huge. Thanksgiving was always good because of the four-day weekend—without adding an extra day of going to church." (Both of us were raised Catholic. Besides going to church *every* Sunday there were many holy-days-of-obligation, extra days of church. Neither of us was that thrilled with kneeling in a pew when we were young.) "You know Hangtime, when I was a kid I was a picky eater. But I always loved the traditional Thanksgiving food. Still do. As a kid, two of my favorite foods, besides ice cream and candy, were turkey, white meat only, and mashed potatoes, white spuds only, no orange sweet potatoes. I liked both served under brown gravy, not white. Pumpkin is still my favorite pie. Glad I outgrew being a fussy eater."

I kept bending Hangtime's ear, "Now, Thanksgiving is my most revered holiday. The day has no religious significance, and there are *no gifts* involved. On Thanksgiving Day it doesn't matter who your god is, or even if you believe in a God or gods. To me, being thankful is one of the best gifts we can give to ourself. Hopefully, Thanksgiving is a day anyone can embrace."

Stepping away from my preachy pulpit, I continued, "There's another reason I love Thanksgiving. It's usually the first day of ski season. As you well remember, in my mid-20s I started working as a powder skiing guide in the backcountry. It was always nice for me to get off my hands and knees while working construction in summer and go to work earning a paycheck skiing fresh snow. Guiding was my dream job."

Hangtime grew up in Kansas, and in the flatlands he learned many games—card games, board games, dice games, all sorts of ball games, and how to fling Frisbees. He was raised by a single mother, and is the youngest of three brothers. Hangtime is fiercely competitive and hates to lose. As a kid, he constantly competed against his older brothers, and usually lost. My theory is that his family makeup contributed to his tenacious mentality.

In my family, I'm the oldest of four siblings and have three younger sisters. When I was playing games with my sisters, in order to keep them interested and to continue playing, I deliberately mis-hit ping-pong balls, mis-played cards, and subtly screwed up to keep a game close. And on a rare occasion, very rare, I even let them win.

During the early mornings and evenings at our camp, Hangtime and I played cards— cribbage, gin rummy, and some ridiculous varieties of poker that he had learned in Kansas, which included lots of extra cards and wild cards. But our favorite style of poker was Texas Hold 'em, like the pros play on television. The two of us would duke it out, one on one, head to head.

We'd also roll dice. Using five, we'd play Farkle and Yatzee. When rolling just two, the game would be Backgammon. Cuss words were cussed, cards slammed to the table, insults were hurled back and forth, none of it in seriousness.

Around camp we'd also played Washers, a game I first learned to play on a river trip. Washers is similar to pitching horseshoes. The advantage to Washers is that washers are easier to carry, and unlike horseshoes if someone gets hit by a washer they're not going to the hospital. Hangtime and I liked throwing Frisbees. We would fly one back and forth to each other or play Frisbee golf. We'd also goof around with a volleyball. In the desert without a volleyball court, net, or people to play with, the two of us simply bumped the ball back and forth. One silly day I got him to play a primitive, Fred Flintstone, style of bowling. I set up "bowling pins," pieces of firewood, and handed Hangtime a softball-sized, perfectly symmetrical, round rock that I'd found on a beach in Mexico and said, "Give it a roll."

On a previous trip to the desert, I had been feeling wackier than normal and convinced Hangtime to climb up a thirty-foot-tall mound of grape-sized river rock. The gigantic pile of small round rock was left over from the construction of Interstate 70. I had a plan about how I wanted to get down—but didn't tell him. When it was time to go, without saying a word, I simply tucked my head between my knees and somersaulted all the way down. At the bottom I thought I might puke. Hangtime also rolled down, and when we stopped roaring hysterically he looked at me, "Batman, you *really* aren't normal."

〜

In camp, at night in the desert, we'd drink a beer or two. Hangtime would sometimes nibble at a Seven-n-Seven cocktail; I'd take thin sips of straight tequila. At this point in our lives we were happy about how little alcohol we drank. Pounding water worked better. We both still love tobacco— too bad for us. In a very distant past we had occasionally sucked on cigarettes, but no more. Hangtime brought a few fine-tasting cigars and offered me one. I declined, but he willingly shared his stogie and let me pull several heavenly puffs. Forget pot anymore, especially the high-tech stuff, it just made us clumsy and slow witted. It also made me paranoid. Any substance more serious was now beyond our juggling capacity. Our lives had more than enough to juggle.

Enjoying the warmth of a campfire on a moonless night and far away from city lights, we admired the star show. Hangtime gazed at the sky, then looked at me and flashed his dork-face. His facial expression let me know he wasn't all that serious when he asked, "Batman what do you think is up there?" He knew neither of us had the answer. Then he changed his mind. "I am curious, what do you think?"

"All I know is that I sleep better under the stars, because looking at them makes my concerns less worrisome. I think it's got something to do with feeling like a speck. It's a big, big place up there." I poked the coals and took another skinny sip and let the strong liquid linger. "I've always thought of the Earth as the cosmic zoo. Our planet has a million forms of life. I'm curious who is visiting the 'zoo' and where they're coming from." Gazing up, I added, "Do you remember the bumper sticker I had on my old red truck that said 'Mean People Suck'? Well that goes for space-beings too. I hope ET, or the aliens, or whoever, or whatever, from wherever, are *nice*. And if I get beamed up into a spaceship full of cattle mutilators, I hope to hell they find the right spot when they probe."

Saturday, with no kids to drag on a death march, we could have hiked long and hard. Instead we sauntered. Because of the short days and with winter closing in, we relaxed in the sun and soaked up as much warmth as possible.

Hangtime needed to head home on Sunday, and he

planned to leave in the early afternoon. I was staying a few more days. On that morning, while the day warmed, more cards were shuffled, dealt, and played. I enjoyed a breakfast-beer and we shared a final stogie. Then we played a casual game of Frisbee golf. For holes, we took aim at sagebrush, fenceposts, rock-outcrops, or anything that worked. Then I said, "You see that black cow way over there?"

"Which one? The one nearest us, with the patch of white on its face?" he asked.

"Yep. That cow's the hole."

Our first throws got us halfway to the "hole." A couple of the herd lifted their heads, when they heard the thud of Frisbees hitting the cheatgrass covered ground. On his next toss, Hangtime, a standout Little League baseball pitcher, let rip a monstrous heave. It was off target, but it skipped between the legs of a startled cow and sent up a small cloud of dust. Mimicking his young son Jason, who can be a prankster, Hangtime shouted, "Made you look. Better yet, made you jump!"

The herd was on to us, and slowly moved away. The two of us followed and kept throwing our plastic discs at them. We started walking faster and faster; the cows did the same. Eventually I said, "If either of us can hit any cow that's good enough." Hangtime sprinted off, running full speed. As it turned out, the not-so-dumb cows kept the not-so-smart humans at a comfortable distance, and we were never able to finish the hole.

$\sim$

When Hangtime had his car loaded and was ready to head home, I told him, "When you start driving I want to get a short ride with you, and then I'll hike back to camp. I think we should go to Golden's. (That's the name I gave the place where I had once found the two electrocuted golden eagles.) You've heard the story but have never seen the spot."

"I've been curious about that place. Let's go there."

Truth is stranger than fiction—and sometimes it is much, much sadder.

Hangtime zoomed up the dead-end road to Golden's. The road ends seventy yards past the highest power pole in the area, the pole where I'd found the pair. Typical of Hangtime, he was hauling butt up the curvy dirt road. His driving has made me nervous one time too many and I often don't like sitting in a car when he's behind the wheel. Sometimes he'll slow down if I gripe enough.

When we zipped past the highest power pole I started wailing, "It happened again! I can't believe it. It happened again!"

"What?"

"There are two more dead eagles."

"No way."

"Yes there are."

"But they changed the top of the power poles," Hangtime said.

Once again, at the base of the power pole, lay two electrocuted golden eagles. We parked and slowly walked toward the tragic pair. *This* was a death march—and I was glad no children were along. Hangtime groaned, "Batman, this is terrible. How could it happen again?"

We were in shock and disbelief. It was a sight neither of us expected. Hangtime said, "I can't believe how strange it is that we were coming to the place where it happened. And that we're here when it happened again." We circled around each of the magnificent beings and looked at both from every angle. "My god Batman, they're huge," he lamented.

Finding the eagles with Hangtime was much different than my first encounter. The first time, both birds looked perfect. Not a feather was askew and their golden eyes were wide open, clear and penetrating. The mated pair was lying together. One's head was peacefully nestled into the other's chest. They looked liked two lovers, who could blink their beautiful eyes, arise from post-coitus bliss and fly away.

But this time the two electrocuted mates ended up eight feet apart. One of the birds was propped up against the bank of the dirt road. It looked perfect. But the other was obviously dead. That golden was lying on its back with its head tilted at an unnatural angle. Most telling, its eyes were "blown," colored an opaque white.

There was another significant difference between the first and second encounter. I wasn't alone. It has been said, *misery loves company*, and being with a dear friend did help soften the horrible blow. Hangtime sat down next to the eagle that looked perfect. After a few minutes, reverently, he very slowly started to open its wing. I couldn't believe the size of the wing, as he extended it more and more until it was fully opened. The underside was multiple hues of brown with white mixed in. Many of the feathers were longer than the combined length of his forearm and hand.

I also couldn't believe that Hangtime opened the wing. The first time I found the pair of goldens, I had only lightly brushed my hand across each one. It was the last thing I did just before I drove away. Hangtime's action broke the ice.

Sitting down within inches of the eagle that didn't look

dead, I touched the point of its talon and pushed to see how sharp it felt. If I pressed hard enough it might have punctured my skin. Then I was curious about the length and placed my little finger alongside it. The talon was about the same length, but thinner, hook shaped, unbendable and stout. They made me think about the claws of a bear, but were not as thick. The three sharp talons protruded from a bright yellow sheaf at the end of its leg. I gently squeezed the sheath and moved a finger up and down it. The sheath was scaly like fish skin, but tough like leather. What a fierce predator. I could see how small game would have no chance, once in its grip.

I ran my palm down its side, from its neck to the end of its wing, feeling the texture of the feathers. Next, I stroked its chest and softly pressed on the puffy layers of feathers to feel the depth of them. During frigid winters in Colorado, I had seen eagles perched in large cottonwood trees along rivers. I now understood how the thick, multiple layers of feathers would provide insulation for warmth in sub-zero weather.

I was becoming a little more comfortable with touching the eagle. I'd started at the tip of the talon— the farthest place from its eyes. To me the eyes were the most intimate part, even though they were no longer capable of sight. I stared into them; they were the most amazing, iridescent golden color I'd ever seen. Staring into its eyes was powerful—yet devastating. This was a rare opportunity, a remarkable gift, but I wished with all my being that it wasn't happening.

Next, I admired and studied the eagle's head and beak. I traced my index finger along the length of the beak and pressed the pointed end. Then I circled my little finger around one of its nostrils. Unlike human nostrils, they were rigid and permanently fixed open; they had evolved perfectly for diving at high speed.

Briefly, I softly caressed the top of its head, the crown feathers. Of all the feathers they were my favorite. The feathers were short, swept back and almost pointed at the end. They had a beautiful lustrous brown color, especially with sunlight filtering through them.

Neither Hangtime nor I wanted to touch the bird that was obviously dead.

The two minutes that I touched the eagle may sound like a science experiment. It was not. Humans in love caress each other. And for new lovers and especially young lovers, their touching is also experimentation. For me, touching the eagle was to experience what an eagle felt like. It was also an act of great love and respect. But my touching was not the excitement of new love, but of sorrow, grief, and loss.

"Mark, this is one of the saddest things I've ever seen. What do you think we should do?" Hangtime asked me.

"I think we need to call the authorities, Dan, so that they know there is still a problem with the redesigned power poles." The top of the pole had been changed between my first and second encounter to prevent another electrocution.

The first time I found two goldens I didn't need to do anything. That time, as I drove away on the dead-end road, a white pickup truck was approaching. I stopped and rolled down my window, intending to talk with the driver. The truck didn't stop, and the stern-faced driver never glanced at me. As the vehicle passed by I saw a government emblem on the door. When I returned to the pole hours later, the eagles were gone.

Hangtime and I said our goodbyes at the deadly pole and he started his drive east. I stayed alone with the pair for a long time. Finally I had to leave and start walking to camp; I wanted to get back before it got too dark. On the hike, in near darkness, I walked to within thirty feet of a black cow with a white patch on its face. It would have been easy to plunk it with the Frisbee in my pack, but I was in no mood for silliness. Back in camp, I wasn't in the mood for dinner either and went to bed early.

When I woke up Monday morning the eagles were the first thing on my mind. While drinking coffee, I tried to find the phone number of the Division of Wildlife in Utah. I keep a couple of different phone books in my truck, but couldn't locate the number. I'm not sure if I was under the spell of the goldens, or what, but I was sick. I spent all of Monday resting, reading, and napping, and never ventured out of camp.

Many Native American tribes use eagle feathers, parts, and entire birds in religious ceremonies. Eagle feathers adorn some ceremonial clothing. A friend who has studied with several shamen of indigenous people in both North and South America once told me, "For some Native Americans, eagles are the most sacred healing tool." I've seen my friend use an eagle feather to fan the air around an individual. Her intention was to both clean and repair their aura, the energy field around the person's body.

Life is gritty at times. Harsh words hurt us, rude and dangerous drivers on the road rattle us, bosses and coworkers can belittle and irritate us, and we even have negative and slimy thoughts about ourself. Those experiences stick to us like dirt. Using an eagle feather to fan the air around a person is like a shower for their soul.

My friend also told me, "Eagles, flying high in the sky, symbolize soaring above the mundane. They broaden our perspective and direct us to look higher." She continued: "They also represent *the initiation of personal power.*" I can relate. The second story I brought to my writers' group was "Eagles on the Highway." After reading that story to the group, despite countless flaws in the story, I felt like I'd hit a game winning home run. Over the years, I often went home from the writers' group a bit discouraged, but that night I went home feeling euphoric.

Adding to my high that night, I got the opportunity to give Karen Chamberlain, the group's co-facilitator, a ride home. Her car was in the shop being repaired. Karen and her husband lived in a very remote place. Before I had ever met Karen, I had lived somewhat nearby to her but less remote. (My place had been three miles closer to town and two thousand feet lower in elevation.) I'd even mountain biked past Karen's distant home. I was the obvious person in the group to give her a ride; I knew the area well, even in the dark.

Karen was considered by many to be a literary wizard. Getting the chance to spend twenty-five minutes alone with her was a thrill and *life-affecting.*

Kind words and encouragement can be very helpful. This is especially true for someone like me, a person who had once struggled with self-esteem issues. Near the end of our drive, Karen told me, "Tonight I heard writing that was technically much better than 'Eagles on the Highway.' But I will *never* forget that story. Just keep writing your stories and you'll figure out the technical stuff later. Write them down rough, and then you can go back months or even years later to rewrite and polish them."

As it turned out, that was the only one-on-one time I ever had with Karen. She passed away from cancer four years later. Karen passed to the other side circled by five women from the writers' group that she'd started. Karen's husband was out of the room at the time. The group members took turns softly reading to Karen during her transition.

The night that I had read "Eagles on the Highway" to the writers' group, I knew my marriage was moving in the wrong direction and was going to end sometime. There was not a lot of drama or anger or tears. My wife and I loved each other, but each of us knew we weren't on the same path in life. Divorce was imminent. For both of us, divorce would be a dream lost.

I'd always enjoyed writing, but in school I hated English. It was confusing, and I was never a strong reader. Back then, I would have rather dissected a stinky wet cow-pie than dissect a sentence to find the noun, verb, tense, personal-pronoun, dangling modifier, and who knows what else. As an adult, free from classroom pressure, I enjoyed writing letters, postcards, and writing in a journal. I'd even roughed out a few stories. During the sad and difficult transition from being married and in love, to losing it, writing helped a great deal to ease the hurt. If there is such a thing as a soul, or a "higher self," or whatever, I felt like it was telling me to write.

Karen's words were great advice. When bogged down and confused by what I call the "paralysis by analysis," I reflected on them often. Finding the eagles had inspired and prompted me to write "Eagles on the Highway." Between that story and Karen's words of encouragement, I could tell I was starting down a new and very surprising path. My life was moving in a different direction. Finding the golden eagles and writing about them was a type of "initiation of personal power."

Since eagles are considered a powerful totem, a medicine man/shaman would probably attach some degree of significance at the discovery of the two golden eagles, especially when it happened a second time. Some signs and symbols are subtle and barely noticeable. But there was nothing subtle about finding two pairs of electrocuted golden eagles. Perhaps what a "white man" like me, a person of French and Sicilian descent, might jokingly, or not so jokingly, call serious juju. Juju or not, Monday when I woke up I was pretty sick and the eagles were weighing heavily on my mind.

~

Tuesday morning I was still under the spell of the eagles, but felt a little better. I hoped that the man in the white truck had come and done his job on Monday. Because of the Thanksgiving four-day weekend, Monday would have been the first workday for a government employee to gather the birds. Perhaps someone else had also seen the eagles and made the call. My only plan for the day was to check on them. I would love to see the goldens again, but much more so, I truly hoped that they'd be gone when I returned.

At noon on Tuesday, I got in my truck and headed to the pair. On the way there, I drove uphill to the top of a small canyon. (The canyon has no official name, but I call it Sage Canyon.) As soon as I crested the canyon's rim, I looked to see if a white truck was parked by the power pole. The deadly pole was a little over a mile away. No white truck. I continued driving, and then turned west towards Golden's and mournfully crept up the dead-end road. If Hangtime had been there, even he would have been driving respectfully slow.

The man in the white truck had not come; the eagles were still there. I parked twenty yards away and grabbed my camera. I walked to the pair and brushed my hand from crown feathers to tail feathers of each, and then started taking photos. After clicking away, I sat for about fifteen minutes next to the one that still looked perfect. The cold temperatures of late November had preserved both of them well. They didn't smell like death. And no flies were buzzing around and no predators had chewed on them. I took a few more pictures and then went back to my truck and pulled out a pad of paper. I dropped the tailgate, sat down, and started writing this story. Didn't make much headway. My heart couldn't find the words; it was too bruised.

After a while I wanted to get out of there. Three weeks before I discovered the first pair of electrocuted mates, I'd seen them perched on the rim of Sage Canyon. I decided to go to the place on the rim where I'd seen the two alive and well. I wanted a reminder of that image—a life-affirming image. I drove a short distance and then walked to the exact spot where I'd seen the pair perched. While sitting there I kept looking at the power pole hoping to see the white truck.

I hiked back to my vehicle, and drove to the beginning of a different dead-end road and started up. The rough dirt road ends at a cliff on the edge of a large mesa. When I got within a hundred yards of the cliff, I saw an eagle take off near the edge. I watched it fly east along the rim of the mesa and drop out of sight. The eagle was either a golden or an immature bald, too young to have white crown feathers. I couldn't tell which. I expected to see it fly above the mesa or soar over the open terrain below and to the south. When the bird did neither, I thought perhaps it might have landed.

I parked at the end of the road, and decided to walk along the edge of the mesa in the direction the eagle had flown. Maybe if it had perched and preened, there was a tiny, tiny chance I'd find an eagle feather. I placed the odds at extremely slim to none. I didn't really care. My only desire was to take a walk and maybe see the eagle again. Plus by hiking along the rim I could keep an eye on the power pole and see if the white truck showed up.

In no hurry, I meandered along the rim. My eyes surveyed the sky looking for the raptor. I also looked at the ground for evidence that the eagle had perched. I searched for a white puddle of pee.* The terrain was undulating and uneven, the gray sandstone pocked with shallow depressions which held a spit of rainwater, and the land was dotted with dark green juniper trees, cliffrose and greasewood bushes. I gave the chances of finding a puddle of eagle pee to be only slightly better than finding a feather. The bird could have landed anywhere on the mesa— if it landed at all.

I walked almost a mile. It would have been easy to miss, but surprisingly, I discovered the "needle in the haystack." Instead of a beautiful eagle feather, I found a very fresh large puddle of white eagle pee. The bird *had* perched on the rim. The puddle also included a perfectly intact turd. Normally,

*Technically, birds do not have urine because they do not have a bladder. Birds excrete both uric acid and feces through their anus.

any bird turd that I'd seen was just a flat black blob in a dried puddle of white pee. Exposure to weather and rain had always broken it apart. This flawless one was only minutes old. I dabbed a finger in the wet white liquid.

How would a Native American react to the finding of fresh eagle pee? They used to build blinds to capture eagles. Teaming together, one would lie in a shallow or dug-out place. The second would cover their partner with vegetation and then place a bloody piece of meat on top of the vegetation, to function as bait. When an eagle landed to take the bait, the hidden person would grab the bird's leg. Native Americans had been around eagles. I'm curious what they would have done with the fresh puddle.

I felt fortunate finding the puddle. In the vast terrain and with the circumstances surrounding the two dead eagles it was a special find. But I had never thought about what I would want to do with a puddle of eagle pee. All I did with the unique opportunity was to dip my finger in the white puddle and take a few pictures.

Looking back, as weird and crazy as it may sound, I wish I'd dipped a finger or two in the puddle and painted a couple white stripes on my face. Then taken a photo of *that*. And for the turd... How many chances do we get to find a fresh puddle of eagle pee with a perfect turd?

After watching the sunset that evening, Tuesday, I headed back to camp. Still no man in the white truck.

Wednesday I needed to return home. I planned to see if the eagles were still at the power pole on my way back to Colorado. Before I left camp to go home, my heart knew the eagles would still be there. Only the man in the white truck, a predator, or a miracle resurrection might have moved the mated pair from their place of demise. I believe in miracles, both minuscule and major, but I wasn't hopeful. Late morning I broke camp and started driving home. When I climbed out of Sage Canyon I immediately looked at the killer pole. No white truck. I drove a bit farther, then turned west and started up the dead-end road. No new tire tracks. I got to the power pole. No predator. No miracle resurrection.

A call would have to be made. Before leaving camp Wednesday morning I'd found the correct government agency. (In Colorado it's the Department of Wildlife, but in Utah it's the Wildlife Resource Division.) I don't know why, but I wasn't looking forward to making the call. Mockingly, I asked myself out loud, "Mark, what is the big deal? You didn't kill them. Or desecrate them. Or anything. You're innocent, the pole is guilty." Both the situation and the fact that I was still feeling a little ill were messing with my head.

I punched the number into my cell phone and then heard, "Hello, Wildlife Resources Division, this is..." Instantly—I liked the kind tone of the man's voice. The sound of it put me at ease and instilled trust. I explained the situation, and gave him the exact location and directions to the pole. I could hear the surprise in his voice when he said, "We've had problems there in the past. But the poles have been changed so this type of thing wouldn't happen again."

Because I felt comfortable with him, I said, "I know. Believe it or not, five years ago I found another pair of electrocuted golden eagles in the same place."

"Really?"

"Yeah."

"Are you there now?" he asked.

"Yeah, I wish you were here and could see 'em."

"I bet they're something special," he said.

"Special, but extremely sad. Makes me want to cry."

"I believe it."

We talked two or three minutes more. After a few seconds of comfortable silence, it was clear our conversation was complete and I said, "Thanks for the help."

"Thank you for calling. You take care."

"You too. It was good talking with you." I touched "end" on my phone and felt a wave of relief.

I relaxed and settled in for my final minutes with the mated pair. Once I drove away—I knew I'd never see them again. I took a few more pictures, including the photo that became the cover of this book.

Many things in life are amazing and powerful, but they are not always wonderful. I've heard it said that contrast is what gives us perspective and appreciation. I am *so thankful* that I got to spend time in the presence of two pairs of golden eagles.

Extra Bits

Where did the man in the white truck take the golden eagles? That question was answered about a year after I found the second pair, when I heard a ten minute radio show on Colorado Public Radio. The program was an interview with Bernadette Atencio; she's the director of the National Eagle Repository, which is where the eagles were sent. The National Eagle Repository (NER) is located in Commerce City, Colorado, a suburb of Denver.

According to Ms. Atencio, who has worked at the repository for seventeen years, the NER receives an average of thirty to fifty eagles per week. The repository receives more bald eagles than goldens. Annually the NER receives around two thousand birds. The primary causes of death are natural causes, road kill, and electrocution by power lines.

After I learned of the repository, I viewed their website. I also found an article on-line from the *New York Times* about the NER. From those searches I learned several things: Protection for eagles began in the 1940s. They are currently protected under the Bald and Golden Eagle Protection Act. It's illegal to possess eagle feathers or any part of the bird without a permit. Many Native American tribes consider eagles sacred. There are 576 recognized tribes who may legally possess eagles. Annually the NER receives 4500 requests for feathers, parts, and complete birds, which is the most common request. The waiting list is 6000 long.

Eagle feathers can last a long, long time after the bird has perished. An eagle has twenty-four large wing feathers and twelve tail feathers. Some Native American families have kept the same feather for generations.

Hangtime with the golden.

Golden eagle that looked perfect, its talons are on the preceding page.

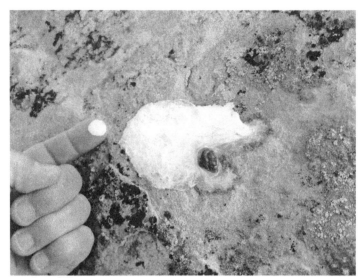

Fresh puddle.

Golden eagle that looked perfect.

Respect and...

Big Water Dan

Slaughterhouse Falls and
Quarterback Dave

Tony, the Human Headpin

Big Water Dan

"Aw, don't worry Mark, you know the Colorado River in the Grand Canyon is nothing but a bunch of big Class III (three) rapids." This pearl of wisdom had credibility. It was delivered not from the mountain top by God's right-hand man, Moses, but almost. The words were spoken at the riverside, by my kayaking coach and guru, legendary Big Water Dan.

Rapids and rivers range from Class I to Class V (one to five). Class I water looks like a lake, it's flat. And in Class V water, an accidental swim could result in a word rafters and kayakers don't like to use—drowning. Most knowledgeable river-people (kayakers and rafters) who have braved serious and scary water, usually know what it means when a rapid is described as having "Class V Consequences."

One fine Grand Canyon day, Big Water Dan was "feeling it." He was feeling good. He was feeling BIG. So after Dan-the-Man had successfully kayaked the toughest rapid in the canyon, Lava, he decided to throw caution to the desert wind—along with his paddle. Below Lava, Dan left his paddle on shore and carried his kayak back to the top of the rapid. At lunch, Big Water had grabbed two round plastic lids from the containers of Pringle® potato chips.

With a Pringle lid in the palm of each hand, he shoved off and headed back into Lava. Basically, Big Water Dan was planning to kayak the rapid using only his hands. His stunt was more for a thrill than hubris.

Lava is the Big-Maa-Moo. The granddaddy rapid of the Grand Canyon. Truth is, Lava is between Class III and Class V. It's on the higher side of Class IV, in my opinion.

So how did it work out for Big Water Dan? Pretty good, I think. He was correctly lined up on the sometimes tricky-to-read entrance into Lava. With his Pringle lids, Big Water was perfectly balanced when he dropped in and started "paddling" down the smooth glassy tongue of friendly green water. Everything was good. But, the River Gods spoke just before Big Water hit Lava's churning, burly maw of chundering whitewater—the tumultuous, surging and folding Vee-Wave. And the Gods only said, "Up yours Little Boy Dan, take a big, big breath of air and have a fun swim."

The monstrous Vee-Wave crashed on top of Big Water and swallowed him up. He disappeared. With only his Pringle lids to brace against the omnipotent whitewater, his craft tipped over. Upside down, the tiny pieces of plastic were of no help as he tried to roll his kayak back up. Out of oxygen, Big Water wiggled out of his boat, found a gasp of air, and swam Lava.

Yep, it worked out pretty good for Big Water Dan, 'cause the friendly River Gods didn't dish out any Class V Consequences.

Slaughterhouse Falls and Quarterback Dave

(This long story about kayaking and rafting is like a multi-day river trip. It takes some time to get from the start to the finish, put-in to take-out. Figuratively speaking, long river trips seem to come full circle, as does this story.)

"Are you lost?" I jokingly asked Quarterback Dave. He had just paddled his kayak over to join me in the small eddy above Slaughterhouse Falls. At this water level, if a kayaker slipped their sleek craft into the quiet piece of still water, it meant only one thing. They were portaging around the eight-foot waterfall forty yards downstream. Dave had been over Slaughterhouse Falls hundreds of times, ranging from water levels so low it was barely boat-able to flows that were monstrously high. I was going to walk around the falls, but why was Quarterback Dave here?

Dave got his nickname because he had removed the facemask from a football helmet and bolted the nose, teeth, and chin-saving device to his kayak helmet. Some boating helmets are lightweight and made with thin plastic, but not Quarterback Dave's. His was the strongest, most heavy-duty model he could find. He wanted the extra protection because of the wickedly difficult creek-runs he had been down; Dave was sometimes among the earliest kayakers who pioneered them. And in a few rare cases, he was the first person to make the extremely challenging first descent.

Floating in the eddy on the right side of the river, I said, "Dave we both know the right side of the falls is un-runable, even for you. There's not enough water. The middle line is really ugly at this water level, if you go there you might need that facemask." The left side was the only clean line. I had never seen anyone aggressively paddle out of the eddy, then zip a quick ferry across the river and run the left side of Slaughterhouse Falls. "Dave what's up? What are you doing here?"

Some gnarly Class-5 rapids and river features have ominous names like Upper Death, Double Trouble, and Lucifer's. Even some "fun and easy" stretches of Class-3 and Class-4 water have unnerving names like Upper and Lower Disaster, Satan's Gut, and Skull, which includes The Room of Doom. Generally, boating anything with the word "falls" in it demands attention. Slaughterhouse Falls didn't get its name because of the nasty consequences that it can and has delivered, but because it's a mile downstream from a former slaughterhouse. The unpleasant place was a mile downriver from the ski-mecca of Aspen, when Aspen was a booming silver mining town in the late 1800's.

The site of the former "house of doomed livestock" is the start of a five-mile section of river named Slaughterhouse. The lively run has countless busy "rock gardens" and six named rapids. According to the biblical guidebook *Colorado Rivers and Creeks*, Slaughterhouse is rated Class-4 at flows below 1700 cfs (cubic feet per second). As the flow increases the run gets faster, "pushier," and much more difficult. At 2700 cfs, it's rated Class-5-minus and over 3700 is a beefy, solid Class-5. Slaughterhouse Falls (SHF) is the most formidable obstacle of the run. SHF—at any water level—is always a Class-5 feature.

Dave and I have paddled together many times since I started kayaking in 1990, but not by design. We're friends, but he's a hardcore Class-5 boater, who often paddles with kayakers of similar skill. I'm a solid Class-4 boater, who ventures into Class-5 only when dragged. By coincidence, usually after work, Dave and I sometimes end up at the same place at the same time, the start (put-in) of Slaughterhouse.

Only 250 yards downstream from the Slaughterhouse put-in is one of the toughest rapids, which is perfectly named Entrance Exam. If a kayaker badly flounders and flails, accidentally swims, or gets really scared and realizes they might be over their head, they might want to consider *not* "passing the entrance exam" and carry their boat back to the put-in and go home. Half a dozen times I've walked back to the put-in myself. On those few occasions, I usually continued to kayak after running Entrance Exam, but by the time I got to SHF I was tired of feeling off balance and thrashing and hacking my way down the river. After shouldering my boat, rather than portaging around the falls, I headed upriver and home. Generally my thought was, *Mark, you don't have it today.*

In Entrance Exam I've seen Dave "slice and dice" through the rapid, paddling back and forth across the river from eddy to eddy, playing in this hole, surfing that wave, shredding the water. Where he enjoyed several minutes of kayaking, it only took me a minute or two. I seldom varied off my proven line, and went from the top of the rapid to the bottom, stopping very little, if at all. And when we got to the falls—Dave always ran.

Over the years, Quarterback Dave has been pretty entertaining. And Slaughterhouse and Slaughterhouse Falls have always been exciting.

～

On my third time through Slaughterhouse, I was standing on shore at the falls and studying the line with my kayaking mentor, Coach. I was trying to find the best line over the falls—and some courage. The first two times I'd portaged. There's an old saying among kayakers when scouting: *If you're too nervous to spit, maybe you should portage.* I was cheating and putting extra liquid into my mouth by sipping on a water bottle. Next, I almost choked when I saw two friends float past. They were headed for the lip of the falls with big grins on their faces. From their *inner tubes*, they both cheerfully waved and yelled, "Hi Batman, surf's up!"

Ignorance *is* bliss. *Screw it*, I thought. If those two yahoo buddies could run the falls, so could I. In a kayak I would hit the lip of the falls with much more speed than the inner-tubers. Fast forward momentum would give me a much better chance to slice through and glide past the ugly reversal at the base of the waterfall. And if the turbulent water knocked me over, at least my roll was reliable. My naïve, inner-tubing friends must have done fine because we never saw them after they disappeared over the lip.

From different vantage points on shore, I tried to figure out the best spot to aim on the jumbled horizon line. A common practice is to follow another kayaker through confusing water. This wasn't an option. If Coach got stopped by the reversal at the base of the falls, I might land on top of him or spear him with my bow when I dropped in.

Coach tried to explain about how many feet off the left bank to aim. He also pointed out a subtle marker on the horizon line, a "rooster tail," a surging piece of whitewater that would sometimes splash up. Slaughterhouse Falls is on a left hand curve in the river. It would be much easier to line up if the run were straight. Coach warned me, "Mark, because the river turns left, when you get close to the lip of the falls the current will push you off line and move you to the right."

Finally, Coach told me to paddle hard towards the blind drop, including the last stroke. This is counter intuitive, because normally when we are unsure of where we're going we slow down, like walking in the dark or driving in fog. It's scary to go full speed into the unknown. There's also added intimidation that comes with knowing what's waiting below the horizon line.

Following Coach's advice, I paddled hard and flew off the lip. Just before hitting the water I closed my eyes. Vision was unimportant. It was also impossible to see because I submerged. In situations like this one, our brain processes information super fast. Even while briefly underwater, I could feel the boat moving downriver. When I began to surface in the chaotic water, I was disoriented and unsure which way to lean or brace. Without a chance for a breath, the maelstrom flipped me upside down. At least I was moving downstream. I snapped a roll and couldn't help but let out an adrenaline-filled scream. Coach exuberantly answered with his distinctive whoop.

One day Quarterback Dave and I were in the S-Curves together, which is the longest rapid in Slaughterhouse. The S-Curves have a large number of big "juicy" holes, places most people avoid. Suddenly, there was Dave directly in front me. He was stopped and playing in a deep ugly hole that I was desperately trying to avoid. I wasn't having my best day and the kayak felt like it had a mind of its own. If I'm going into a bad hole, unplanned and unwillingly, I subscribe to the best strategy which is generally: *When in doubt, straighten out, point downriver, and paddle like mad.* But there was Dave.

Rather than hit Dave with the pointed bow, I turned sideways and fell into the hole. It happened fast. I wasn't sure if I had landed on top of him, or what. Seriously flustered, I tipped over. Somehow I washed out of the "sticky" hole and rolled my boat right-side-up. I was bummed and disappointed in my inept river skills. More importantly, I was worried about what type of harm I might have done to Quarterback Dave. When I looked around for Dave, I saw him upstream— he was still playing away in the same ugly hole like nothing had happened.

Minutes later, embarrassed, I paddled into the eddy where Dave was resting. I was afraid he was going to be pissed off. Before he could verbally punch me, I said, "Quarterback Dave, if I'm going to slam into anyone you're the *best* person to hit." Through his facemask he gave me a funny look. I kept talking, "You've had more weird crap happen to you in a kayak than anybody I know. Better to run into you, than someone less experienced. Sorry Dave, glad I didn't hurt you."

Quarterback Dave graciously accepted the strange compliment. "Batman, don't worry, you only briefly interrupted me. By the way, nice roll."

~

Water hydraulics: What makes a waterfall so dangerous? It is not being crushed by the weight of the water, but being trapped in the endless recirculation of water in the pool at the base of the waterfall. Sometimes the victim is not only trapped, but is repeatedly pushed underwater by the cascading water. No one can swim forever, even with a lifejacket.

Water wants to level itself. When dense water pours over the lip of a waterfall, the column of water penetrates into the pool below and makes a depression: a "hole." The surrounding water in the pool rushes in—to fill the void—where the column has pushed down. This creates a type of wall, or current, around the hole which can trap a swimmer. The victim cannot swim over, or through, the wall of inward rushing water. If a person is trapped, the best hope of escape is to swim down toward the bottom and try to find a way out.

Waves, holes, and wave-holes (a wave with a peak that is folding back upstream) are river features that make a river become alive and exciting. The surface of a river is predominately determined by the river bottom: especially by large rocks or boulders near the surface. When water flows down the spillway of a dam the surface of the water is smooth, despite the steep drop and high speed, because the spillway is made of smooth concrete.

The speed of the river also affects the surface, to a lesser degree than the bottom. Imagine hitting a speed bump in a car at 10 miles per hour, that's no big deal. But hit the same bump at 65 mph and that's much different. The steeper the river, the faster it flows. (Gradient is a term to describe the steepness of a river.) Riverbanks also have an effect on the surface. When the banks constrict and tighten, because of converging current, the water gets more jumbled and its speed increases.

Waves are pure pleasure, and a wave-train (a series of waves with peaks and valleys) can be whitewater bliss. Early in my boating days I was scouting a Class-4 rapid with a friend who was comfortable in Class-5 water. The water was hauling-butt fast and looked kind of chaotic, munchy, and intimidating. My buddy helped me analyze the rapid piece by piece. His advice was "Mark, look at that line more or less down the middle. Basically it's all big waves. Some are breaking and crashing more than others, but none of them will stop you. And most likely—if you keep paddling—they won't flip you. My advice is to aim for the top of the waves and go for the big ride." I pointed at the huge pour-over hole at the end of the wave-train. He said, "Don't worry, you'll see it coming and you *will* miss it." All good advice. After running the rapid we eddied out and carried our boats back to the top and ran it again. Pure adrenalized fun.

Holes are different than waves. Holes can be really fun—or not at all. Most of them are formed by a large rock or boulder in the water, or by a shelf or ledge. The hole is on the downstream side of the rock, because the river has poured over a rock or shelf. Sometimes you can see the rock and other times it's submerged, but you know it's there because of frothy white water on the surface. Some holes can have a similar component to waterfalls, a column of water penetrating into the river. They're known as a pour-over hole, usually shortened to just "pour-over." A bad pour-over would be a keeper-hole, which is a difficult place to get out of. The characteristic of a hole—which is also sometime called a reversal—is white water folding and crashing upstream onto itself.

Smallish pour-over hole in Slaughterhouse. Fish like the calmer water out of the main current, downstream of the submerged rock. Note: fish jumping out of the river.

Holes vary in size, from as small as a bus tire to being as big as the entire bus. Not all are mean and nasty, some have a "friendly" shape. Deciding if a hole is a place to play or to avoid like a landmine, depends on one's skill level. What determines if a hole is friendly for an expert kayaker? First, how easy will it be to get out once they drop in? Second, will the hole rip their arms off? Experts look at how deep the hole is and whether there's a "soft spot" on the surface. The middle is usually the deepest part. But one side or the other might not be as deep and it's easier to work their way out. Swimming out of a hole is a desperate option and would be considered a rotten last choice. A kayak is kind of like a balloon full of air on the water; it floats. If a kayaker is stuck in an extremely bad hole, they can pull the nylon loop on their spray skirt and "pop the balloon." The boat will fill with water and hopefully wash out of the hole.

All this talk about pour-overs and keeper-holes. In twenty-five years of kayaking, only once have I been out of my boat in a bad pour-over. It happened my first year of kayaking in a Class-3 section. I accidentally went over a pour-over, flipped upside down, and couldn't roll. When I swam out of my boat I was stuck in the hole. Five kayaker friends watched from a nearby eddy. Because water surges, some hydraulics change for an instant or two. But not always. After about 90 *very long* seconds, something changed on the surface and I was able to swim away. My boat stayed another ten minutes, before it catapulted into the air and out of the hole.

From that experience, I learned that being upside down is not the worst thing that can happen. When someone is learning they're going to get knocked over, especially if they try more challenging water. But being upside down in your kayak and *not* moving downriver is something you don't want. That means you're stuck in a bad hydraulic.

In years of boating, I've only seen one kayaker who was stuck right side up in a wicked hole and needed to pull their spray-skirt to get out. It happened in Slaughterhouse, in a rapid named Triple Drop. I was floating in an eddy fifteen yards from the hole. I've kayaked past the deep, ugly, ledge-hole a hundred times and always missed it. A few friends haven't been as fortunate. And who was the kayaker who *intentionally* paddled into the Triple Drop Hole, used his full bag of tricks to try and get out, but eventually needed to pull his spray-skirt? Quarterback Dave.

Avoiding the "nasties" in the river is what river people do. They learn to read the surface of the water. Sometimes rafters and kayakers stay in their craft and read it on the fly, "read and run." Other times they get off the water and scout. They study the rapid from shore to determine the best line. Waves are often glassy green water, versus holes which are aerated white water. Finding the smoothest line through a tough rapid, "the green highway," is often where boaters choose to run. (There are other things to avoid in rivers, but that's later in the story.)

Waves, holes, wave-holes, pour-overs, and keeper-holes—waterfalls are in a class by themselves. Slaughter-house Falls, at a height of eight feet, might not seem very tall. But the sound alone can be in intimidating. It's a force to reckon with, a place to respect.

Author running Slaughterhouse Falls, around 1,000 cfs.

On Quarterback Dave's 40th birthday, I too got a special gift. He and I joined a large group of kayaker friends and went to my favorite piece of Class-3 water, sublime and exciting,

Westwater Canyon. Westwater is on the Colorado River in the Utah desert, just a few miles west of the CO/UT state line. Before getting to the put-in, I had no idea Dave would be on the trip. And until we got to the spin-hole above Marble Canyon Rapid, I had no clue it was Dave's 40th birthday.

Dave and I started the trip wearing big straw hats to hide from the blazing sun and the 100-degree heat. Our helmets were clipped to the grab loop at the stern of our boats. Quarterback Dave wore a colorful, short-sleeve Hawaiian shirt for additional protection; I relied on my Mediterranean olive skin and paddled shirtless. This was a heavenly change from wearing four or five layers to keep from turning blue on the frigid Roaring Fork River at home. Midsummer, the temperature of the Colorado River was a tropical 78 degrees, but the color wasn't a tropical clear-blue, but its often murky chocolate-milk-brown. Totally relaxed, Dave and I each had an open beer tucked into the top of our life jacket.

The first significant play spot is the famous Little Dee Hole, where Dave shined. Anyone can fall into the hole in the middle of the river on their way downstream—if they want to. Just line up and drop in. After the first simple chance to drop into Little-Dee, one needs to make a difficult ferry from an eddy on river-right to get into the hole. A few of us weren't sure we wanted to complete the ferry. Especially as we got closer to the deep, powerful hole and got a better look. One could take a weak last stroke, rather than the strong one, which was needed to drop into the thumpy place. Then you could pretend you weren't afraid, but just couldn't make the move. Dave made the ferry every time.

Back in 1995, playing in a hole was called "hole riding" or "rodeo boating." Rodeo boating, because it was like being on the back of a bucking bronco. There were a lot of great kay-akers on this trip, and the Little Dee rodeo started. A bronco rider at a rodeo needs to stay on the horse eight seconds to score points. In rodeo boating, a measly eight second hole-ride would be lousy and non-scoring. A high scoring ride needs to be dynamic, exciting, and lengthy; one can't just stay in the hole and do nothing. No scores were formally kept. But from the volume of those cheering from the eddy and the others eating lunch on shore, it was obvious who was scoring huge points. Dave would have been a contender for top prize. No big deal, we'd seen him do this before.

If Quarterback Dave shined at Little Dee, when we got to the second play spot, the spin-hole above the Marble Can-yon Rapid, he could have been named Hollywood Dave. He blazed in the spotlight. Dave decided to do forty consecutive flat spins, also known as 360s, to celebrate his fortieth birth-day. Today's kayaks are designed to spin, it's much easier. But back then, to spin a boat and not tip over or wash out of the hole required good skills. *No one* stayed in a hole and did forty consecutive flat spins.

"Give it a go Dave, try for forty. I'll count for you," a woman on the trip told him. A group of us patiently waited our turn and watched him from an eddy, as he linked 360 after 360—forty of them. If it hadn't been Dave's birthday, one of us would have started blowing their rescue whistle, barking at him to quit being a hole-hog. But it was his b-day, plus none of us had ever seen anyone do forty flat spins in a row.

Downriver at Sock It To Me, if one decides to go into the surging, inconsistent, raft flipping wave-hole—it's like sign-ing up for a car wreck. Little skill is required for the "head-on collision." Just eddy out next to the crazy hole and paddle in. Then get *trashed*. Mostly likely, you'll get spit out upside down and definitely disoriented. The gutsier the boater, the more car wrecks they sign up for. Quarterback Dave's auto insurance would have been canceled.

At the bottom of Last Chance, the last rapid in Westwater, our boating friend Henry was the prima ballerina—he out-danced everyone. He completed double pirouette after double pirouette. Henry correctly lined up and poked his bow into the precise spot of the pour-over, which pushed the bow down and made his kayak stand vertical. Then, "standing on point," the toe pegs in his boat, he took a perfectly timed stroke across his bow and started spinning. Henry spun not once, but linked two rapid revolutions. He must have tried thirty-five times and successfully completed fifteen or twenty. Single pirouettes could be accomplished by mortals, but the only person I've ever seen do a double pirouette was Henry.

By the time they reach Last Chance, many kayakers are spent after a hard day of boating and only dabble there. Especially knowing there are still six miles of flat water left to paddle. Most of us relaxed in the eddy. Dave and Henry didn't stop playing or rest, and the two of them were last to head downriver.

In the guidebook, *Colorado Rivers and Creeks,* Slaughterhouse is described as: *Its teeth have definitely been pulled.* This means that the Roaring Fork no longer reaches huge water levels. Several upstream water diversion projects are the reason. Forget about teeth. In the summer of 1995, with the river rising following a banner snow year, Slaughterhouse began to grow fangs. And on the morning of July 12th the fangs had morphed into the monstrous jaws of a great white shark. At nearly 7000 cfs, the Roaring Fork was devouring riverbanks, chewing and tumbling boulders, and chomping on boats and *boaters*—Class-5 with extra serious oomph.

1995 was my fifth season as a kayaker. 1994 had been a dream year. I kayaked about eighty days, twenty of them in Slaughterhouse. Some of those days were at a good-sized flow, maybe up to 2500 cfs. That year I rolled a couple hundred times, and a few of those rolls were in miserable places to be upside down. It seemed like a miracle, but I never swam that year. In '95 my kayaking season started in the Grand Canyon. It was my first trip down the Big Ditch as a kayaker. I was ready and Coach was along which was really helpful. We had a great trip and I even rolled twice in the toughest rapid, Lava. Nerves got to me the first time and I just tipped over on something minor. When I rolled up, I saw a huge wall of water and thought *I'm going to get crushed*. Which I did. But I rolled again. Despite having kayaked burly rapids in the Grand Canyon—by July of 1995, the extreme high water in Slaughterhouse had scared me away.

The morning of July 12, 1995, the Roaring Fork could have been renamed The Raging Fork. That day, the water diversion projects upstream of Slaughterhouse were dry; their long tunnels bored under the Continental Divide, which deliver water to the Eastern Slope of Colorado, were empty. The high mountain reservoirs east and west of the divide were full. Everyone's thirst was fully satiated, no water was being diverted. Every drop of H_2O that belonged in the Roaring Fork drainage was heading that way. The Roaring Fork River was back to its former self. Look out!

On my way to work the morning of the 12th, I stopped at the bridge near the Slaughterhouse take-out to look at the river and check the gauge. The gauge is nothing sophisticated, just simple horizontal stripes spray-painted in one-foot increments on the concrete bridge abutment. Next to the stripes are numbers, also in spray paint. I had been religiously checking the gauge every morning. I'd also been calling Water Talk. (Colorado and other states have a network of river gauges. You can make a phone call and punch in the appropriate numbers and a robotic voice will give you the CFS at the site you want. The info is updated about every four hours. River flows are also available on-line.)

During my previous morning stops to look at the gauge, I hadn't seen any kayakers. But on the 12th there were three cars parked at the take-out with boats on top. I could see people moving gear and getting ready to drive to the put-in. Almost certain that I would know them, I drove up to say hello. My Lazer was on top of my truck; that's where my kayak lived during boating season. I found four kayaking friends, Quarterback Dave, Kelly, Donny, and Henry. Each of them were gnarled veterans, solid Class-5, or 5-Plus boaters. The "Raging Fork" was within their skill level. Although I'm certain even the big boys were feeling butterflies in their stomach, well maybe not ice-cool Kelly. He and Donny had kayaked flows that big in 1984. Henry, fearful that the river might start dropping and not wanting to miss the peak, was dashing around like a hummingbird that had been gulping at a feeder full of Red Bull.

I got out of my truck, "Morning guys. Biggest day yet."

They barely mumbled hello and not one of them looked at me. I knew why. They were afraid I wanted go with them.

Each stayed busy moving gear, which was a perfect excuse to avoid talking to me. I had parked next to Henry's classic, 1967 blue Chevrolet Chevelle, and he had quickly ducked out of sight behind the other side of his car. Silently, I watched them for a while, as they shuffled gear and loaded boats on top of one vehicle. They continued to avoid eye contact. It was kind of humorous watching those fearless kayakers squirm in a socially awkward situation. They knew Slaughterhouse at this level was a risky, big step up for my skills. But no kayaker wants to tell another boater, *you can't come with us.*

Finally I stopped their wiggling-about, "Don't worry, I *don't* want go. Nothing bad has happened this season. But I got scared away from here a few weeks ago, when the river got too big for me. I'm just looking at the gauge." The mood instantly changed and we started talking.

Kayaking Slaughterhouse at 7000 cfs is instinctive. There's not a lot of time to think. Reading and running: the mind quickly reads the water, and the body reacts and makes the moves. Once the four launched, it was like being on a screaming fast freight train and you're along for a big, big ride. In Entrance Exam, the first rapid, there was *no* playful paddling back and forth across the river from eddy to eddy, nor shredding the water. The holes were huge and mean. And at that water level there were almost no eddies, just a few places along the shore where the river was a bit slower.

Years later, Quarterback Dave described the run to me, "It was hard to see in places because the peaks of whitewater were so tall. It helped a great deal that I was *very* familiar with Slaughterhouse. I knew from memory, more or less, what was coming. The key in '95 was getting in Slaughterhouse early and staying with it as it got higher and higher."

Donny's description, "It was all hairball."

They arrived at the scout above SHF in no time. Donny once told me, "When we were at the scout, it all looked pretty ugly. The left side was awful and the hole on the right side looked bad." Normally at high water, the run was hard-right, only a few feet from shore. But at 7000 cfs that line wouldn't work. Dave, Kelly and Donny decided to portage; Henry wanted to run.

At 7000 cfs the best line was in the center, a "thread the needle" move from right-center to left-center. It was not a line Henry had ever tried. Henry's plan was to hit a seam in the mayhem, a weak spot between the left side and the right side—and blast through at full speed. SHF had different plans.

Adhering to standard river procedure, the three who were portaging set up "safety" for Henry, in case his run didn't go well. Quarterback Dave and Kelly waited in their kayaks near the base of the falls. Donny stood on shore. He was on the edge of the steep hillside that dropped straight into the river. Donny was only a few feet from the hole on the right side. The ground was loose, so he had secured himself to a tree. Donny was ready with a throw-line in his hand.*

---

*A throw-line is standard boating equipment. A kayaker's throw-line is 50 feet of line, 3/8 of an inch in diameter. The line is carefully tucked into a nylon bag. The bag has a piece of foam floatation stitched into it and is designed to float. If Henry needed help, Donny could hold the end of the line and throw the bag of rope, which would uncoil as the bag flew to Henry. Henry could grab the bag or rope and Donny would pull him to shore. Rafters carry a throw-line 100 feet long and 1/2 inch in diameter.

Henry paddled hard on his line toward the lip of the falls, with serious and focused determination. Unfortunately, SHF had more stopping power than Henry had speed and forward momentum; he was unable to "punch" through the seam. The reversal at the base of the falls grabbed Henry and his boat.

Donny had an unbelievable, close up view of Henry's wicked two minute hole ride. Years later Donny told me, "After what seemed liked forever, Henry's spray skirt must have popped off, because his kayak washed out of the hole. But Henry was still in his boat." The instant Henry got out of his kayak, Kelly was right there and swooped in to help Henry to shore.

Quarterback Dave chased Henry's boat. Once Kelly got Henry to shore, he also pursued the plastic. They quit the chase after about a mile, because of a low pedestrian bridge by the Aspen Airport Business Center. The bridge is usually not a problem, but the river was so high that they couldn't safely get under it and had to stop. The low bridge was a blessing. Guilt free, Dave and Kelly could let Henry's boat go downriver. Almost every kayaker has their name and phone number written on their paddle and kayak. Henry got his boat back later that day; it was stopped and pulled out of the river by a kayaker who was paddling fifteen miles downriver near Basalt.

Hazards in the river: The primary things to avoid in the river, in addition to bad holes, are manmade objects and downed trees. A manmade object would be a barbwire fence, low bridge, old dam debris, culvert, water diversion apparatus, low-head dam, concrete blocks with exposed re-bar, junk cars, or any big trashy thing that was dumped in the river. To me, downed trees are probably the worst hazard. They're known as "strainers," because the river flows through tree branches, but an object can get tangled and stuck in the strainer. A strong current can relentlessly hold a boat or boater against a downed tree until the river drops or rises, which can be days, weeks, or even months later.

Manmade objects, bad holes, and waterfalls are fixed in place; they don't move. Even some downed trees have been in the same place for decades. Strainers move around—especially during high water. A new strainer can happen in the blink of an eye. Trees grow old and fall into the river. Strong winds or heavy snowfalls bring trees down. The river can undermine a tree's root systems and instantly there's a new strainer. The most commonly asked question by someone boating Slaughterhouse, or any mountain river, for the first time of the season is often, "Have you seen any new wood in the river?" I've seen warning-notes posted at a put-in, giving the location of a particularly bad new strainer.

A big rock in the river might look intimidating, but the water "pillows" off of it. This means that the water bounces off the rock and creates a pillow of whitewater. Depending on one's comfort level, some pillows are friendly and fun to bounce off of. Others are about as user friendly as resting one's sleepy head on a block of granite.

Railroad tracks and roads often parallel rivers, because the river has carved the easiest route through mountains and valleys. Rivers tend to have a natural boating pathway, of sorts, which is a main channel where most of the water flows. In the early days of railroad and road construction, before environmental concerns, a lot of jagged boulders ended up in many rivers. As a result, some rivers now have big ugly jagged boulders in the natural pathway.

Slaughterhouse doesn't have large manmade rocks. But the run does have a gnarly object in its path, which was possibly made by man.

One day I was portaging around SHF and saw a longtime, well-known Aspen couple walking along the Rio Grande Trail by the falls. The Rio Grande Trail is the former railroad bed between Aspen and Glenwood Springs. The husband said to me, "You know Slaughterhouse Falls is manmade." I immediately stopped walking and gave him a puzzled look. I'd never heard that before. He continued, "When the railroad was built in the late 1800s the river's original course was changed. It got moved farther to the left, against the base of Red Butte."

The husband, who was easily recognized by his radiant smile, started pointing things out. He showed me that the railroad bed had been built by filling part of the area with rocks and boulders. This saved building a bridge, and kept the track in a straight line. He also pointed out a large pond at the base of a steep hillside where the river once ran. What he said made sense. I don't think many people who walk or bike the Rio Grande Trail realize that Slaughterhouse Falls is most likely manmade.* And no one with whom I've kayaked Slaughterhouse has ever mentioned it.

SHF is a Class-5 feature, in a section of river that at low to moderate flows would be a Class-4. As I said earlier, I've

---

*The course of the Roaring Fork River was definitely affected during construction of the railroad bed. To what degree, I'm not sure. My research is ongoing. See photos pages 224-225.

never relished Class-5. I've never loved running Slaughter-house Falls; sometimes I'm more comfortable than other times. The fact that SHF is waiting downstream is always in the back of my mind and pit of my stomach. For me, and some other boaters, paddling Class-5 is retro-fun. After you do it you're glad you did, but I can do without the nervous anticipation.

Kind of an odd coincidence: two days after Henry lost his kayak for a few hours, I lost my kayak for almost two weeks. I had a close encounter with a spruce tree that had fallen into the Roaring Fork; it happened just upstream from Ba-salt. The tree must have been in the river for years because it had no branches. That was a good thing; there was less to get tangled in.

In fast moving water, I got surprised by a shallow gravel-bar in the middle of the river. I tried to move left of it, but when my boat hit the gravel-bar I got pushed to the right. I didn't even see the log until it was only a couple of feet away. With no time to do anything, I leaned on the tree and dropped my paddle to put both hands on the log. Instantly, I flipped upside down. It all happened in seconds. Fortu-nately I washed under the log and was able to get out of my boat. I ended up stranded on the gravel-bar island in the middle of the raging Roaring Fork.

A television crew from Denver had been filming in Ba-salt for three days. The newsworthy event: extreme high wa-ter had washed away part of the original highway. (When first built, Highway 82 was two lanes. Years later the high-way was moved to the opposite side of the Roaring Fork and four-laned.) The morning of my island experience, I noticed the crew had gone back to Denver. Lucky for me. Because the film crew would have had plenty of time to move their cameras, and I would have been looking bad on statewide television. I could imagine the anchorperson saying, "Near Aspen, a crazy kayaker is marooned on an island, in the middle of the flooding Roaring Fork River."

I was stranded for almost an hour. In that time a dozen people gathered on shore. A boating friend lived nearby, and somehow he'd heard that a kayaker was stuck on an island and he showed up with his throw-line. My three kayaking companions had also walked upstream when they realized I was missing. My buddy heaved his throw-line. It was too short and we didn't connect. He carefully repacked the yellow line back into the bag, and we moved closer to each other. More failed attempts. The swift current kept sweeping the line out of my reach.

The two of us finally connected, only because I'd kept wading deeper into the river. At the moment both of us connected, I had one chance to jump into the river and swim for the throw-line; just an instant to grab the line or face a long, long swim. Once I got hold of the throw-line, the current straightened the line and swung me *almost* to shore. I had to let go of the lifeline and stroke the last few yards, while people screamed, "Swim hard!" One of my kayaking partners grabbed me while I was face down in the water, still stroking.

Eventually I got my kayak back, never saw the paddle again. Someone had found my boat but couldn't read the faded writing inside. I was reunited with my boat when the guy who found it asked some kayakers by the river if they knew who had lost a boat. For the first week after my island misadventure, I didn't miss my kayak *at all*.

~

Although I've never heard it used, my guess is that the Roaring Fork River's full name is The Roaring Fork of the Colorado River. During the huge runoff of 1995 I remember kayaking to the confluence in Glenwood Springs. That day, according to Water-Talk, the Roaring Fork was 11,000 cfs which was larger than the mighty Colorado River at 10,000 cfs. That was unusual, because the fork of a river is almost always smaller than the river it flows into. Because of dams, water diversion, and irrigation, it's impossible to know what the true, unaltered, flows of each river would have been that day. Only the hydrologists who control the water have a clue.

Before people started manipulating its water, the Roaring Fork roared for thousands and thousands of years. And its granite river rocks and large boulders have been tumbled and well-polished into smooth round shapes. Kayakers, and especially rafters, love rocks without jagged, raft-tearing edges.

Commercial rafting companies and a few private boaters run Slaughterhouse when the river has enough water—but not too much. Rafters use only paddles. Slaughterhouse is too narrow and dotted with rock-gardens and boulders to have two oars extending beyond the rubber.* It's good en-

---

*Rafts are controlled by using either oars or paddles, or sometimes a combination of both. Oars are generally 10 feet long. They're attached to a metal oar-frame, which has been strapped to the raft. Sitting in the center of the raft, one boatman will row using a pair of oars. Paddles are about 5-6 feet long and are handheld. Anywhere from 2-8 people will paddle a raft. The raft-captain sits at the stern, barking commands.

tertainment watching rafts snake their way through and pinball off the round rocks. Invariably some rafts will get stuck. It's only temporary. The raft-captain will move around in the boat to shift the weight, or if the water is shallow they'll jump into the river and try to work the boat off. My favorite technique that rafters employ to free a broached boat, is when they play bumper boats. A raft moving downstream will intentionally bump, or semi-slam, into the boat that is stuck, in order to knock it free. It's impressive watching a *skilled* raft-captain and paddle-crew negotiate the river.

When commercial rafters get to Slaughterhouse Falls, they don't portage. Rafting companies often hire a kayaker to go with the group and safety-boat. Their job is to "fish out of the drink" anyone who gets bounced out of the raft. It's a high-risk, low-paying job. Actually it's not too dicey in Slaughterhouse, because commercial companies go only at moderate flows, when the river is Class-4—except for Slaughterhouse Falls. Part of the safety boater's job is to run first at the falls, and be waiting and ready.

For anyone running SHF: it's always an eye-opening thrill. Slaughterhouse Falls doesn't discriminate. It doesn't know, or care, if you are paddling soft rubber (raft), paddling hard plastic (kayak), or dog paddling with your hands in an inner tube—the place treats everyone the same.

$$\sim$$

In the way that Quarterback Dave and I, *unplanned*, occasionally ended up in the same place at the same time, my friend Bob and I ended up in the same place at the same time—and neither of us wanted to be there. But considering the alternatives, we were pretty darn relieved about our predicament.

After work one day at the Slaughterhouse put-in, eight kayakers spontaneously became a single group. We all knew each other. Everyone was a solid kayaker, no rookies or baby-boaters, and we were all familiar with Slaughterhouse. QB-Dave wasn't there. When we got to SHF, no one felt like they needed to scout and no one was portaging. Each of us was running the falls. That day the run was on the left side of the river. The left riverbank is a steep hillside of gray shale. The only question: how many feet from the left shore to run? The range was from three to ten feet.

The running order was free flowing. No huddling up and making a plan. About eighty yards upstream of the falls, a few of us pulled into the shallow slow-moving water on the right shore. I got out of my boat and dragged it a short distance from the river, so I could stretch my legs and sponge the cold water out of my leaky kayak. I also wanted to watch and see where each kayaker hit the horizon line above the falls; I was the least experienced boater. Bob, a gray-haired friend and gifted kayaker, also got out of his boat. Coach ran first. He didn't eddy out, but stayed in the middle of the river and ran. On his way past, Coach looked over at us and smiled and shouted his distinctive whoop.

Below the falls, Coach eddied out on river-right. Staying seated in his boat, Coach signaled us when it was clear to run, so we'd know that no one was caught in the reversal at the base of the falls. His signal was simple. Coach extended the end of his paddle into the air as high as he could reach.

The remaining kayakers either stayed in the middle of the river and ran, or briefly stopped with Bob and me and then went. He and I were the last to go. Before Bob paddled away, we talked about which line to run. Both of us decided to run hard-left, close to shore. The advantage to the line was that we could stay out of the more turbulent water. The disadvantage became obvious within minutes.

While standing on shore, it seemed like a tiny bit longer than normal before I saw Coach's signal that it was clear to go. I didn't think much of it. I was focusing on the horizon line and trying to decide exactly how far off the left bank of shale to aim. In prior runs, I'd been experimenting with different distances. My last image was of Bob's stern going out of sight over the lip.

With my boat still on shore, I spun it around so it was facing the river and squeezed in. Then I wrestled the tight fitting spray-skirt into place and laid my paddle across it. I adjusted my nose plugs and took a few deep breaths. Using both hands, I pushed off the small round river rocks and slid my kayak into the moving water. Quickly, I grabbed my paddle. Then I refocused on the horizon line and took a couple of light strokes to get lined up. The horizon line comes up fast, and in seconds I was paddling full speed toward the blind drop.

Just a few feet from the lip of the falls, the bottom of my kayak scraped *hard* on shallow shale. I never saw it. It was like hitting a deep patch of sand on a mountain bike. I lost almost all of my speed, and fell off the lip with no forward momentum. Instead of gliding through the ugly reversal, I dropped straight down into the maw and flipped upside down.

Tons of water thundered down next to me. The sound never changed. I was stuck in the reversal. Fortunately, I wasn't directly under the pounding water or behind the waterfall, yet. I thought about setting up to roll. But after 10 or 15 long seconds, I quickly decided that I might need every molecule of oxygen to escape the reversal. I pulled the loop on my spray skirt and wiggled out of the boat.

I surfaced in the tumultuous, swirling pool of water at the base of the falls. The sound was like an endless freight train. The view was an unnerving, in your face, close-up of the waterfall only a few feet away. Over the years, I'd heard a little bit about being sucked back into the column of pounding water and getting stuck behind the falls. I back-paddled with both arms toward shore, and *never* looked away from the waterfall.

I was lucky, and moved a few feet farther from the cascade. Then I glanced over my shoulder to see how close I was to shore. My brain was already disturbed by the situation, and then it became confused by what I saw next—a kayak paddle in the air. Paddles don't fly, they float. I turned around to make sense of it all and saw my buddy Bob. He was standing knee deep in the small eddy at the base of the falls, the Postage Stamp Eddy. He was holding the blade of his paddle and extending the other blade for me to grab.

I back-paddled harder and kicked towards Bob. A few more strokes and his paddle was within reach; I rolled over and grabbed the end of it. Just then, my kayak floated by and I lunged at the grab-loop on the stern. With both hands full, I kicked and Bob pulled me toward him. As soon as the water was shallow enough, I stood and stepped closer to him. I never let go of Bob's paddle or my boat. The instant I was close enough, Bob put a vice-grip hold on my PFD (personnel flotation device) to steady me, and we stumbled out of the river.

Bob's a cool head under pressure. He once owned a large construction company in the Midwest that employed hundreds; he'd seen plenty of things go wrong. The Postage Stamp Eddy is not a serene piece of still water. It's a squirrelly place, where the wild water surges up and down. Bob and I had been together in the eddy before, but always *in our kayaks* after successfully running the falls. We had eddied-out there by choice. It's an exciting place to watch your friends fly off the lip, and if something goes wrong you're right there to help.

This time Bob and I had a problem. Bob had his paddle, but no kayak. I had my kayak, but no paddle. The hillside of shale is really steep next to the Postage Stamp Eddy, so one can't get out of the river and walk up or downstream. The only exit out of the eddy is by kayaking or swimming. We needed to get across the river and join our friends; plus they might have our missing gear. But the two of us had only one boat and one paddle. The solution was simple.

Swimming in Class-4 water is *much* more reassuring if you're holding the grab-loop of someone's kayak and they're towing you. In the past, I'd heard Bob say "If you are going to laugh about it later, you might as well laugh about it now." With that philosophy in mind, he smiled and handed me his paddle. "Looks like you're driving. Driving your boat with my paddle. Batman, give me a good ride."

Bob and I knew that the worst part was over; the ferry to our friends would be no problem. We also knew it could have gone much, much worse when each of us dragged the bottom of our kayaks across the shallow shale at the lip of Slaughterhouse Falls.

Once again I found myself in the Postage Stamp Eddy. This time I had my boat *and* paddle. I was sunny-side-up and everything was fine. I floated in the surging eddy waiting for Melanie, a friend who was running the falls for just the second time. Melanie is a gutsy woman. Courage has nothing to do with gender, and if Melanie were male she'd have gonads the size of coconuts. Portaging was not in her vocabulary.

Earlier we had scouted SHF. When I mentioned the dry-hair option, walking around the falls, Melanie wanted no part of it, "I've watched lots of people run the falls. I'm ready." But I don't think she was quite ready for the run she was about to have. Neither was I.

"Okay, do whatever you want," I told her. "I'll try to get into the Postage Stamp Eddy after I run. If I make it, I'll wait for you there." I aimed a little farther left than I had been running, so I'd have a better chance to catch the eddy. But not *too* far left. Success. I bobbed up and down in the loud surging eddy, staring up at the lip. Then I saw the end of Melanie's boat, but something didn't seem right. Before my brain figured out what was wrong, I saw Melanie in her kayak—she was facing upriver. Somehow she had run the falls backward. My mind groaned, *Oh crap.*

Miraculously, Melanie sailed past the reversal before flipping upside down. My next thought: *Oh, things are looking a little better. She's only upside down and not upside down stuck in the falls.* I whipped out of the eddy and followed her. I made sure not to get too close; I didn't want to get in Melanie's way when she swept her paddle across the surface of the water and started to roll. Melanie snapped a solid roll, looked at me, and then shook her head and started laughing.

I paddled up to her. "I wish I had a camera. You're the only person I've ever seen run the falls backward. What happened?"

"I got too close to the left shore. The slow water next to shore grabbed my bow and turned it. Then the faster moving water, farther from shore, caught my stern and spun me around."

"I don't think you'll ever let that happen again."

"Never."

$\sim$

My first kayaking experience with Quarterback Dave was a little unpleasant for me. I'm certain he doesn't remember it—but I've always tried to remember the point he made that day.

Coach and I were in Shoshone, a Class-3 section on the Colorado River, seven miles upstream of Glenwood Springs. Coach was leading the way. We pulled into a large eddy on river-left and found seven kayakers floating in the eddy. They were waiting their turn to play in a wave-hole. Coach knew everyone and I knew most of them. QB-Dave was there too. It was only my fifth day as a "real" kayaker, someone who has their own gear.

Prior to that day, I'd paddled a few times, but had never owned a kayak nor had the skill to roll it. But in March of 1990, at Coach's suggestion, I took a rolling class offered by Colorado Mountain College. Coach lent me his gear. The class was four weeks long and met twice a week, eight sessions. Best of all, in addition to the two excellent instructors, the classroom was the "World's Largest Hot Springs Pool," in Glenwood Springs. The water was a comfortable, student-friendly, 94 degrees. Learning to roll a kayak does not come naturally. But by the end of the class I'd learned how to roll. It wasn't "bomber" by any means, but I could roll and understood the mechanics.

After the class I started the process of ingraining the roll into my muscle memory. Five hundred practice rolls seems to be the minimum, and more like one thousand are needed before it's firmly ingrained. Rolling in a pool or flat water is one thing, but being upside down in a moving river is another. When you get knocked over in the river—you want to instinctively act—not have to think a lot. Once upside down, one needs to wait patiently until their body is in the correct set-up position—then quickly snap a roll. Patience, yes. Panic, no. This isn't always easy, because breathing underwater is impossible.

Later that spring, after the class, I went on a five day flat-water river trip on the Green River in Utah. Every day I did at least 40-50 rolls in the cold river. After the river trip, I drove to Lake Powell and paddled near shore and practiced for three days. Back home in Colorado, I did a few more rolling sessions in a swimming pool. By the time I went kayaking on a moving river for the first time, with Coach and a group of baby-boaters, I had a solid roll but was untested on anything but flat water.

During our first day together, Coach watched me do lots of practice rolls and then roll for real when I tipped over while playing. Coach is a former Outward Bound instructor and familiar with helping people find the upper limit of their skill-level. On our third day together, Coach and I went to the South Canyon Wave with one of his friends. They surfed the wave. I just tried to ferry back and forth across the fast moving river. I got turned upside-down about fifteen times, but managed to roll.

Coach and I went to Class-3 Shoshone on our fourth day. Coach felt confident that if something went wrong and I had a bad swim I wouldn't give up kayaking. Plus he knew I'd been knocked around bodysurfing in rough ocean surf, so I was fairly comfortable in water. Kayaking is a head-trip sport. I know more than one person who has had a bad experience kayaking and *never* got back in a boat.

On our fifth day together Coach and I were back in Shoshone, where we ran into Quarterback Dave and a group of kayakers floating in an eddy. The boaters were waiting their turn to play in a wave-hole. I rested in my kayak and watched them play. Quarterback Dave paddled over and we exchanged a few pleasantries. Then Dave pointed at a surging mass of whitewater, just twenty yards downstream from the wave-hole where the boaters were playing, and said, "Mark, you could drown in that keeper-hole right there."

Like a frightened three-year-old would run to their mother and cling to her leg, I paddled over to Coach. "Dave told me I could drown in that keeper-hole. I don't know what a keeper-hole is. But I understand drowning!"

"Relax, Mark. You aren't going to die with a large group of big-boaters so close by. Being in Shoshone on your fifth day of kayaking might be considered too much for your lack of experience. Plus you don't look that nervous for a baby-boater. I think Dave wants to teach you a lesson about having respect for the river."

∿

Underestimating the power of the river is sometimes easy to do, because most often everything goes okay or only mildly amiss. Alright, sometimes it gets pretty messy. But in every trip that I've been on the injuries have been minor and everyone survived. Not all the gear survived. Successful runs, naturally and thankfully, lead to confidence.

Unfortunately, success sometimes also leads to overconfidence and complacency. The "spankings" the river hands out are generally not too severe—a miserable and frightening swim, or cuts and bruises. Lost gear is unfortunate, but not that important in the big picture. I've seen kayakers take great risks in crazy water chasing an empty kayak, when at that point I considered it to be an insignificant piece of plastic. A "bad beat" would be a dislocated shoulder, broken bone, or injury to the face. Drowning is very rare. But it does happen as rafters, and especially kayakers, venture more frequently into extreme water. Boating Class-5 is always risky. The balance between the "beats" and successes keeps the majority of people in check and for the most part respectful.

~

Traveling full circle and back to the beginning of this story: I was floating in the eddy above Slaughterhouse Falls and getting ready to portage, when Quarterback Dave paddled into the eddy. Teasingly, I asked him, "So Dave, what are you doing in this eddy? Are you lost?"

"Batman, I'll walk with you. I'm portaging."

"Dave, are you hurt? Do you need a hand with your boat?"

"Mark, I'm fine. Slaughterhouse Falls has been very,

very kind to me over many years of kayaking. Every day of this boating season, so far, I've walked around the falls. I am showing my respect to the river."

Quarterback Dave is Dave Eckardt, co-author of "Colorado Rivers and Creeks." The book was first printed in 1995 and is still the "bible" of boating in Colorado. Some of the photos might be considered dated because of the old boats. But the pertinent information is still invaluable and prized, because while kayak design has changed significantly, the put-ins, take-outs, and most importantly, the rivers, have not changed that much.

In my experiences with Dave, I've found him soft spoken and modest. During his epic kayaking career, he has spent countless days kayaking Class-5 water. Dave also has seven first descents. Quarterback Dave has never swum at Slaughterhouse Falls.

$\sim$

Sad ending: Henry in this story is Henry Filip. Henry died kayaking on the Crystal River near Redstone, Colorado, in June of 1997. He was in a Class-5-plus section named Meat Grinder. Henry had paddled the section many times. He was paddling alone that day, but three boating friends were watching him from shore with throw lines. Under extremely difficult circumstances, Henry could not be saved. He was 38 years old.

Quarterback Dave and Henry had paddled together often. Henry was a phenomenal kayaker and skier. He was short in stature, but his presence was huge. He had an unforgettable toothy smile and unique loud laugh. Henry defined enthusiasm and intensity, his wonderful nature was infectious.

Henry's memorial was held at the Slaughterhouse put-in. Sometimes when I'm paddling alone in Slaughterhouse, I pull into a quiet eddy and talk out loud to Henry, as if he were floating in his boat next to me. A pair of Henry's ski boots hung from a tree at the top of a steep run on Aspen Mountain, the 1A Lift Line. Recently the ski boots were replaced by a memorial plaque. Filip's Leap in the Highlands Bowl at the Aspen Highlands ski area, is named in memory of the amazing man so many of us loved.

Dave Eckardt.

Henry Filip.

Extra Bits

Kayak design and shape have changed radically over the last twenty years. Each year the boats get smaller and smaller. While kayakers still run long sections of river and go on multi-day river trips, a big part of the modern era of kayaking is about whitewater parks and "park and play." This means driving to one spot on the river—parking there and then playing—doing tricks in tiny boats. Sometimes there is a short section of river with several features to play in.

Prior to whitewater parks, skilled kayakers were always surfing waves and playing in holes. Back then, the bow and stern of old-school boats were fairly symmetrical and shaped the same. Then kayak designers started making the stern smaller, which gave it a lower volume of air. The small stern made it easier to get out of a hole and more maneuverable while playing. Some kayaks are now designed specifically for whitewater parks.

More and more communities have started spicing up a "drab" section of river by placing boulders in the water, creating river features. The city of Glenwood Springs spent over a million dollars building a whitewater park on the Colorado River. Construction involved much more than simply placing boulders in the river. The Glenwood Whitewater Park has hosted the U.S.A. National Freestyle Team Trials several times. Freestyle kayakers do all sorts of tricks, and use boats so tiny that their kayak can fit inside a car.

Henry doing a double pirouette in
Westwater Canyon. Photo: Doug Lee.

Glenwood Springs Whitewater Park hosted the U.S.A. Freestyle Kayaking
Team Trials. Just minutes after the competition ended, several competi-
tors shared the wave. It was a friendly free for all. This was highly unusual, because boaters compete or play on the wave one at a time.

"Not all the gear survived..." The author and David G., both baby-boaters at the time, went to Class-3 Shoshone. David tipped over, couldn't roll, and swam. The kayak's cockpit caught on a pointed rock and the boat folded. Big-boater David Powers, paddling alone, came to the rescue. He towed David G. to the kayak. Once out of the river and in the sun for a few hours, surprisingly, the boat returned to its original shape. But its structural integrity was destroyed and it was never the same. David Powers' helmet can be seen above the rock. Author purchased photo from a company that took photos of rafters in Shoshone.

Grand Canyon 2009, left to right, Jules Campbell, author, Kevin Frazier, Andy Putnam. Great skill sometimes trumps modern equipment. Jules went into huge gnarly ugly places in his large old kayak; hydraulics that most boaters would *always* avoid. Then he carried his boat upstream and did it again and again. Jules started kayaking when he was seven years old, and both of his parents are Olympic caliber kayakers.

Slaughterhouse Falls is out of character for the Roaring Fork River. Downstream of Aspen—except for SHF—the riverbed is all tumbled round rocks, *no ledges or waterfalls.* In the late 1880s, two railroad companies were racing each other to build the first rail-line into Aspen, which was a booming silver mining town of 10,000.

My guess is that because of Red Butte, the river ran around the end of the butte and farther to the right, where there is now a large pond. In their haste, rather than build a bridge, the Denver Rio Grande Railroad definitely filled some of the area for the railroad bed, and they might have removed some of Red Butte. These two actions, filling and perhaps removing part of the butte, affected the course of the river and moved it to the left. This quite possibly created SHF.

Google Earth image: Roaring Fork River, marked by parallel white lines. Slaughterhouse Falls marked by a small white circle. The Rio Grande Trail is to the left of the river. The author believes the river once flowed where there is now a large pond. The large pond is left of the Rio Grande Trail and marked by a white line.

Photo from 1890. Left to right, railroad bed, SHF, and end of Red Butte. Railroad construction was completed in 1887. Note the absence of large trees, unlike today. Photo courtesy of Aspen Historical Society.

Photo circa 1900. Left to right, railroad bed, Roaring Fork with SHF, and Red Butte, which dominates the photo. Maroon Creek is far right. Note: at river level, the end of Red Butte was possibly removed. Photo courtesy of Aspen Historical Society.

Tony, the Human Headpin

Lifelong best friend Dave Johnson, DJ, and I started trundling as kids, rolling discarded tires down what we called the "Cowhills" east of San Francisco Bay. Most of the tires we found were just bald black rubber, without the metal rim. But once, we found a tire that not only had its rim—it was fully inflated. Oh my, that tire was our most memorable trundle because it bounced crazy-high when it careened out of sight down the golden hills of dried grass. We were squealing with delight. Our glee quickly ended when we realized the tire might not stop until it hit someone's house. If we caused any damage, we never heard.

We also trundled rocks. We would roll any size rock we could get into motion. DJ's fascination with rolling things became his sport. As a kid he loved bowling. Tall and athletic, DJ participated in all the traditional sports, but the out-of-the-mainstream sport of bowling was his favorite. In the Cowhills he searched out bowling-ball-sized rocks, and would take aim at a distant oak or bay tree, pretending it was the headpin. The headpin is the most important pin in bowling. It is in the middle of the bowling lane— front and center in the triangle of ten pins. Each pin has a number and the headpin is number one; it's the focal point of all bowlers.

One of DJ's early birthday celebrations was a bowling party. The biggest kid there was also named Dave, but unlike my wonderful best friend that giant ugly kid was a bully.

The mean jerk gloated, after he "bullied" down five-dozen defenseless pins, for the highest score of sixty. DJ knocked down forty-nine, second-best score. I rolled a five. Yep, five. Smallest kid, tiniest score.

In the years since my pitiful game, the saint protecting small shrimpy kids invented bumpers. Today no kid rolls a measly five, because bumpers are placed in the gutters at the sides of the bowling lane. Now, instead of a non-scoring gutter-ball being "down in the dumps," it bounces off the self-esteem-saving devices. The ball will tap down a few pins, but probably not all ten. At least there's action and something fun happens no matter how weak and unskilled the bowler. Funny, but my favorite/lucky number is five, but it has nothing to do with my low-scoring game.

Years later, at another bowling birthday party for DJ, his parents suggested he open his gift before the game started. Dave unwrapped a heavy package to find his very own bowling ball. That was a cool gift. I can't remember the color but it wasn't black, which was unusual because back then almost all bowling balls were black.

DJ continued to bowl all his life. He and his wife participated in bowling leagues. One night I got a late call, "Marco, you won't believe it..." Scoring 300 is a perfect game, rolling twelve strikes in a row. A strike is knocking down all ten pins with one roll. Perfect games are rare, and especially rare for amateurs. DJ had thrown nine strikes in a row when he stood up for his final frame—the tenth.

DJ told me, "Marco, there was a large crowd watching. A buzz had circulated around the bowling alley that I had a perfect game going." In league play, the running score of each player is projected, frame by frame, above the bowling lane. "The crowd kept growing. I was in the zone, sitting quietly alone between frames, sipping nothing but water."

To complete the perfect game, DJ would have to roll three strikes in the tenth frame. His first roll was a strike. The automatic ball return delivered his sixteen-pound ball, and he lined up for his next shot. It was also a strike. Now he had thrown eleven strikes and needed only one more for a seldom-seen perfect 300.

"I focused on the headpin and got ready for my first chance at a perfect game. As soon as the ball rolled out of my hand, I *groaned*. I had pulled the ball to the left and completely missed the headpin. I couldn't believe it. I knocked down only five pins and ended up with a 295." Dave was always extremely good natured. Years later he told me, "Batman, I'm just glad that once in my lifetime I had a shot at a perfect game."

DJ gave me a wry smile when I told him, "Think about this, more people have rolled 300, 299, 298, and 297 than have ever bowled 295. A score of 295 is much rarer than a perfect game. And think about this, we are probably the only two friends—in the world—who ever have collectively bowled games of 5 and 295. And by the way, if you add my worst game of 5 to your best game of 295, together our scores make a perfect 300." We were a lifelong perfect match.

Damn, the saddest day and biggest gutter ball of my life was the day I learned that Dave passed away. All his life, until the day he died, he remained true to himself and loved by all. At the end of one's life, what a great compliment to be described as: "Loved by all." In addition to wonderful parents, having a lifelong best friend like DJ was the greatest gift I ever received.

~

Just as DJ had continued bowling all of his life, I continued our bad habit of trundling. Occasionally I'd roll a rock in the mountains of Colorado or off a desert cliff in Utah. I trundled for pleasure. Then one day, I found myself rolling a bowling-ball-sized rock down a steep avalanche path. I was trying to determine if the slope was free from avalanche danger and safe to ski. Trundling with a purpose.

I wanted to find out if the snow I was tempted to ski was hard or soft. If the avalanche path was firm, most likely the slope was safe. Springtime is the safe time to ski steep, avalanche-prone slopes, after the snowpack has gone through several days of a melt-freeze cycle. This means the snowpack has softened during warm sunny days, and then re-frozen solid on cold clear nights.

To understand how the melt-freeze process makes a steep slope safe to ski, think about a tray of ice cubes. When the ice tray is first filled, the water will run out if it's tipped just a few degrees. As the water in the tray starts to freeze, the top becomes a thin layer of ice. The tray can be tipped a little more, and the fragile layer will hold the remaining water in place. But if the tray is tilted to a steeper angle, the weight of the water will break the thin ice and pour out. The longer the water freezes, the thicker and stronger the ice becomes. Finally when all the water is frozen, the tray can even be turned upside down and the ice will remain in place—it's solid.

I wanted to be sure the avalanche path I was looking down was like a frozen ice tray, or at least that the top layer was solid. Sometimes it's difficult to look at snow and figure out if it's hard or soft. A simple way to determine the snow's density was by rolling a rock down the avalanche path. If the rock skipped and bounced down the steep slope, the top layer was probably frozen hard enough to be safe. If the rock stuck in the snow or rolled only a short distance before stopping, the slope was too soft. So by rolling a rock—without entering the avalanche path—a risk-free decision could be made.

The avalanche path I was peering into was Keno Gully, or simply Keno. Keno is on the western edge of the Aspen Mountain ski area in Colorado—*outside* the ski area boundary. The half mile long avalanche path is easy to look down; it's only a hundred feet from the top of the Ruthie's ski lift. The run can be extremely enticing.

Officially, the ski patrol calls Keno Gully "Ophir" because Keno sits on an old mining claim named Ophir. In the last ten years, a small ski patrol shack was built just a few feet from the top of Keno Gully. Because it's out-of-bounds, the ski patrol does little or no avalanche control work in Keno.

A couple of asides about Keno: Legendary ski mountaineer, Lou Dawson, once broke his leg skiing Keno Gully. After his incident and rescue, Lou wrote an article for *Powder* magazine entitled "Out of Bounds and Out of Luck". He later became famous in the backcountry skiing world for being the first to ski all fifty-four of Colorado's 14,000-foot mountains. Lou has since authored several guidebooks.

Once, while guiding a snow-cat skiing trip on the backside of Aspen Mountain, I started talking about Keno Gully with one of the clients, a local named Benny. He seemed pretty self-assured, bordering on cocky. Benny told me that one time he'd skied Keno in three feet of waist deep powder snow. He said, "It was the *best* run of my life. It was so good my friend and I went back to ski it a second time." Benny and his buddy must have had angels skiing with them that day.

Before the start of their first run down Keno, Benny had called a taxicab. The cabbie waited near the bottom of the Keno and then shuttled the two back to the base of the ski area. Benny and his buddy then rode the 1A ski lift and the Ruthie's lift back to the top of Keno. Benny told me, "When we got back to the top of Keno Gully and looked down—the *entire* gully had avalanched." If his timing had been a little different, it almost certainly would have been the last ski run and last mistake of his life.

~

The first time I skied Keno Gully was with a friend named Rob. We were in our early twenties, young and inexperienced. I wanted to be sure Keno was frozen solid. Trundling a rock seemed the safest way to determine the stability of the snowpack— primitive but effective.

Finding a rock at a ski area is not always easy, they're covered in snow. With the idea of skiing Keno in mind, I had looked around earlier and found the right sized rock. It was in a protected place, on the lee side of a small ski-lift building. I wrestled the bowling-ball-size rock out of the snow. Then I had to ski one run and ride the Ruthie's chair-lift holding the gray orb. I was comfortable skiing with the rock cradled in my arm. I wasn't so comfortable trying to explain the inevitable question, if asked, *"Why are you carrying that rock?"*

Standing on the flat terrain above Keno Gully, I gently

pitched the rock over the edge. It skipped and then bounced out of sight, well over a thousand vertical feet. The snow was solid.

Keno is not a place for a skier or snowboarder to fall—it's very, very steep. From the level ground at the top, Keno immediately changes to 45-50 degrees. At the start of the run there were a few "trippers" that we needed to avoid. These were a couple of rocks that were barely exposed and also a few small sticks of vegetation poking out of the snow. I *especially* didn't want to screw up the most important and difficult turn—the first. A person who fell might cartwheel and slide a long way before stopping.

It was my idea, so I went first. I side-slipped around the rocks and twigs, and cranked a good turn. Then I breathed. My gulp of air was followed by fifteen or twenty conservative turns, before I stopped and looked uphill. When I quit turning, Rob cautiously dropped in and linked solid strong "bomber turns." He was a ski racer. Once together, smiles were exchanged because the crux, the hardest part, was behind us. But Rob and I remained guarded; the slope was still really steep. We continued to ski one at a time and kept an eye on each other.

Someone else had also been keeping their eyes on us, my roommate Holly. She was waiting on Castle Creek Road near the bottom of Keno Gully and had been watching us with binoculars. Holly had my car and planned to give us a ride back to town. She also had beers, because if everything went well we were hoping for a late morning, mini-celebration.

When the angle of the slope eased, Rob and I relaxed. Frolicking like two playful kids released by the school bell and dashing to their favorite hangout, the two of us linked our turns together all the way to the bottom. With me in front, Rob's ski tips were on my tails. Elated, the three of us each enjoyed a celebratory beer, while standing on the roadside looking up at Keno. Keno Gully had been an excellent and thrilling adventure.

~

Over the following years, I skied Keno once or twice a season. Some years I never skied it because the snow failed to go through a melt-freeze cycle. Many days I longingly looked down Keno, just because, even when there was no possibility of going. As my avalanche forecasting skills improved, I was tempted to ski Keno in powder conditions when I thought the slope was safe. A few times I even saw other people's ski tracks in the fluffy powder snow. But I resisted temptation.

One year the melt-freeze cycle happened earlier than normal. That year, I skied Keno Gully for the first time in late March. I'd gone solo. Keno was perfect, and three days later I was back again. I started skiing it a lot, perhaps ten times that season. No rocks were ever trundled. I was tuned in to the cycles of the melt-freeze snow. Sometimes I'd ski it with a friend or two, but never with more than three of us total. About half the time I went by myself. But if I went alone, I *always* "checked out" and told a friend where I was going. Then I'd check back in as soon as possible and let them know I was okay.

Skiing alone—outside the ski area boundary—is considered a big no-no, for obvious reasons. If you get completely buried in an avalanche, it's 99.9 percent certain you're going to die. Sadly, this has happened to more than one friend.

And if you fall and get injured… But at least by checking out, I eliminated the risk of not being found for days or even hours. Plus I tried to ski conservatively. Mentally I shifted and went into a mode I called "great-great-grandpa-goes-skiing." And like a 108 year-old man would tentatively walk down a stairway, I tried to *slow down*, and focus on each turn. I also tried to temper my exuberance. My body didn't always accomplish this. It's a little like promising yourself to always use a condom, but then exuberance happens. Yet every time I'm skiing in the backcountry, I change my brain to a more guarded mode.

One year, after the ski lifts closed for the season, I hiked to the top of Keno Gully. It was the same year that I'd skied it about ten times. I was alone and the snow was suspect, so I trundle-tested the slope. The rock didn't roll, but stuck in the snow. The snow was too soft and I simply just skied away. I never tempted fate. I skied Keno only during the melt-freeze cycles.

Over the years Keno Gully had become a familiar place. I felt like a lucky guy with a generous lover. I always treated Keno with respect, and never took her for granted. Keno had always been sweet, kind and thrilling.

∼

Pete was a young co-worker and friend; he and I had made a plan to ski Keno Gully. It was going to be Pete's first run there, and it had been about fifteen years since my first. Pete had the day off, but I needed to work until noon. We had arranged to meet at the bottom of Aspen Mountain, a few minutes after twelve.

That day, Pete was also planning to ski with his pal Tim

in the morning. Pete had asked me if Tim could join us in Keno. Tim and I had skied together a little. He was a solid skier and seemed very sensible, so I told Pete, "It would be great if Tim wants to come along. Most of the time it's safer going out-of-bounds with three skiers rather than two."

When something goes wrong in the mountains, often it's because little things start adding up. While it can take hours for the things to stack up—the moment it all goes wrong is often instantaneous.

"Hi Pete, sorry I'm late. You know how it can get at work." Then I added, "It's already pretty warm, the snow in Keno might be too soft." The first two things, warm weather and being late, were starting to stack up. We hurried towards the gondola, for a thirteen minute ride to the top of the mountain. Now a third factor was in play—being in a hurry. A fourth issue was also in the mix. Tim had brought an unknown friend, Tony.

Over many years of backcountry skiing, I had become particular about who and how many people I went with. Too many skiers increase the odds of something going wrong. But *who* I was skiing with was much more important than how many.

As a ski guide I'd seen some risky, cavalier, and just plain dumb things done in the backcountry. Sometimes it was a wild and impulsive move. I, too, had made some less-than-perfect decisions, but so far I had been fortunate. Most of the problems I encountered had to do with a person's attitudes—a lack of respect for the mountains.

Tony had the look of confidence. He wore snappy clothes and carried himself with an air of self-assurance. As we hustled to the gondola, Tony gracefully glided in his heavy and stiff ski boots. The boots are designed for skiing at high speeds, not walking. I've had seemingly flawless days of skiing, only to slip on the ice and splatter in the street walking back to my car at the end of the day. Tony made walking in those clumsy, Frankenstein-slippers, look easy.

The four of us loaded into the gondola car. We were the only people in the car, and once we settled in I repeated my earlier concern: "We may be too late to ski Keno. The day is already warm, and the snow might be too soft."

I knew both Pete and Tim had never been down Keno. I asked Tony, "Have you ever skied Keno Gully, aka Ophir?"

"I've ducked under the ski area boundary rope a few times. But I've never heard of Keno Gully or Ophir." Then I knew for sure, I was the guide/leader and primary decision maker.

Our conversation turned to where the three of them had been skiing, and a little about the snow conditions. They'd been on the double-black-diamond runs, the most difficult slopes on the mountain. From the conversation, it sounded like Tony was a really good skier and confident, which was good to hear. What was unnerving though, Tony sounded *eerily* like Benny, the cocky ski client I knew, who had come close to being killed in Keno. Tony was confident, but he too seemed to border on cocky.

Our gondola conversation should have included more of a discussion about the snow conditions, such as, what was the snow like where the three had been? I suggested that we at least go to the top of Keno and take a look. I said, "I'll probably go down only a turn or two, and see how the snow feels. If it's too soft I can hike back up."

I can't remember for sure, but I think Tony might have

said, "We'll be okay."

Tim wanted to go into the ski patrol room on top of the mountain and get their opinion. I had been a ski patroller on Aspen Mountain for two seasons. I was in a hurry and didn't want to spend any more time talking with the ski patrol and let the snow get softer.

My buddy Pete is the youngest of eight siblings. He is a quiet, soft-spoken guy who doesn't say much. But when he does speak, he's one of those people whom others listen to. Despite Pete's youth and lack of backcountry experience, I wish I had asked his opinion about the snow conditions and skiing Keno. He is a sharp kid.

Intuition has been referred to as "the sixth sense." People use it in every aspect of life. Some of us hear it louder, and heed it more, than others. Famous mountaineers have acknowledged the value of honoring their intuition: Sometimes it can be as simple as, *I've got a bad feeling*. My intuition wasn't flashing a "red light" and saying, *Don't go with Tony*. But when we stepped out of the gondola car my intuition was definitely blinking a yellow warning.

Standing on the flat terrain above Keno, the four of us peered down. It was first time that season that I'd stood on top of Keno Gully with the idea of skiing it. Unfortunately, when we skied from the gondola to Keno I hadn't been able to get a good feel for the snow conditions. And being in a hurry, I hadn't wanted to take any extra time to look for a rock and trundle-test the slope. It would have been *the* perfect time to bowl a rock down Keno.

Before dropping in, I repeated the directions a final time. They were as crystal clear as the Colorado sky: "I'm only going to ski down a few turns. Then I'll move into the aspen trees on the left side. Stop in the trees. *Don't* go below me." Straight down the main alleyway of Keno there is not one tree. The seedlings have been torn out by avalanches. But there is a grove of aspen trees on the left side of Keno Gully, and below that, a forest of large spruce trees. Trees are almost always the safest place to wait. The bigger the trees, the better, especially thick spruce.

I made five turns and ducked into the aspen trees. The snow was soft, but I stayed on top of the surface. Tim, savvy and smooth, light and soft on his skis, prudently started his descent. He also stayed on top of the snow, and stopped close by in the aspens.

Tony weighed a little more than Tim or I, plus his skiing style matched his personality. Tony pounced into Keno Gully and pounded the slope with hard, harsh, aggressive turns. His heavy turns put ruts in the snow, four to seven inches deep. *Uh-oh,* I thought to myself. *The snow is much too soft. It's not safe. We'll have to hike out.*

The safe option disappeared when Tony skied past Tim and I, and kept going and going and going. Finally he stopped, 150-200 yards below us—where he stood dead-center in the middle of Keno Gully. If Keno Gully had been a bowling lane, Tony would have been the human headpin. Now I was *extremely* nervous. I didn't want to panic. Nothing had happened but I knew the situation wasn't good.

Tony was barely within earshot. I yelled his name, and gestured with my arm and ski pole for him to move out of the gully. Tony remained oblivious, like an unconscious, inanimate wooden bowling pin. He never paid attention to, or perhaps never saw, my wind-milling arm and ski pole. He was looking all around, but he seldom looked uphill.

Keno Gully was like a tray of ice cubes with just a thin fragile layer on top. Tim and I had only scratched the surface. But Tony had cracked it with the ruts he carved. Pete was the last skier. He dropped in but made only two turns before he stomped hard on the brakes and jammed to a stop. Pete was alarmed by something he saw.

The snow in Keno Gully was tender and fragile. Only a very delicate tension had been holding the snow in place, and Keno could not tolerate any more jostling. Pete was the trigger, "the straw that broke the camel's back." When Pete started to ski, the weakest part of the slope cracked open just below him. Tons of dense, heavy, gloppy snow ripped out and started avalanching.

Fortunately, Pete had seen the crack in the snow the instant it opened, which was why he stopped. Luckily for him, he was above the avalanche fracture line. When Pete stopped, he was fine. Tim and I, waiting in the aspen trees, each of us on the uphill side of a large tree, were also okay because the avalanche was in the gully, not the trees. But Tony, standing dead-center in the middle of Keno Gully...

I had also seen the crack the moment it happened. When the snow broke open, time shifted to a different dimension —super slow motion. While Pete was turning to an abrupt stop, my mind screamed, *Avalanche!* Then it seemed like *f-o-r-e-v-e-r* before my mouth started working, "Avalanche! Tony, avalanche, move left!" Then again, "Tony, avalanche, move left!" I didn't stop hollering until Tony looked up. In the seconds this was unfolding, my mind raced through several scenarios, all of them terrible.

If Tony didn't move the result would be horrific. Tony was facing to the right, so he skied to the right. The left side of Keno, near Tony, was a thick forest of large spruce trees which was one hundred percent safe. The right side, where Tony had moved to, was out of the main avalanche path but was a treeless, open slope. The snow where Tony was standing could be "sympathetic." Which means that because of the avalanche in Keno, the snow where Tony was standing could be disturbed enough that it would also start avalanching.

The unstoppable freight train of concrete-like snow tore down Keno Gully, and scraped away almost every bit of snow down to the ground. The snow where Tony was standing stayed in place—not solid—but solid enough. The avalanche ran 1400 vertical feet and about a half mile.

I looked up at Pete and yelled, "Pete, do you want to hike out of here?" The answer was obvious and he climbed up the slope. Tim and I would have done the same, but neither of us ever thought of leaving Tony.

Tim and I cautiously descended. The "ski" down to Tony was terrible. We negotiated our way over big hard chunks of frozen avalanche debris, old stumps, dirt, and rocks. When the three of us got together no one said much. We were stunned. We were also humbled.

We continued "survival skiing" to the bottom, over the same awful conditions. We just tried to get down without trashing our skis or getting hurt. No exuberant turns were made. Keno was ruined for the season.

I've always said, "One of the best things about getting older is *hopefully* getting wiser." In those brief minutes we all matured years, and gained or regained, a lot of respect for the mountains. When this incident occurred I was thirty-nine-years-old, oldest, and by far the most experienced. I should have known better—about a lot of things. Thankfully no one was killed.

Keno Gully.

Boy trundlers.

Acknowledgments

I would like to thank the current and former members of the Glenwood Springs Writers' Workshop (GSWW). Without their—lovingly given—highly skilled, literary guidance this book would not have been possible. First I would like to acknowledge the two founders Karen Chamberlain and Carol Bell. Thanks to the current co-facilitators/leaders, Pat Conway and Debbie Crawford, who skillfully and graciously lead the group. A special mention to George Lilly (a woman) who reviewed a number of the stories outside of the group setting. Current and former members of the GSWW in alphabetical order: Noel Armstrong, Stanley Badgett, Anita Bishop, Kristin Carlson, Liz Colter, Gayle Embrey, Pat Girardot, Donna Gray, Jim Gisburne, Francie Jacober, Corrie Karnan, Tana Leonhart, Connie Noel, Claudia Putnam, Don Rogers, Joyce Yoder and Zell Zordel.

Thanks to Dan "Hangtime" Keener, Sam Cox, Steve Vanderleest, Dave Eckardt, Padraig Allen, Steven R. Williams, Steve Wight, and Tom "Cardo" Merrill who were willing to let me share their stories.

Many friends read some of my work and gave their input: Lisa Amador-Di Mento and Paul Di Mento, Rhonda Armburst, Janette Logan, Alan Arnold, Carol and Walt Smith, Lee and Jules Miller, and Marie Warren. A special mention to Richard Warren, who read every story and made meticulous notations which were extremely helpful. Rich also proofread the final draft.

For technical support I'm grateful to geologist Garry Zabel, and also archivist Megan Cerise at the Aspen Historical Society.

Numerous dear friends helped in ways they may not even realize: Thomas Lerner, Andy Collis and Tammie Albers, Bert Przybylski (Sh-bell-ski), Dave Lofland, Vince Galluccio and Gayle Hayes (deceased), Mick Shattuck and Joannie Haggerty, Stephanie Johnson (DJ's widow) and a group of friends collectively named "The Bobs."

Thanks to my three younger sisters and their spouses: Michele McAustin, computer help; Mitzi Mortimer, editing assistance; Renie Gannett, test reader. I would like to acknowledge my mother, Ann Batmale, for a lifetime of countless pearls of wisdom and help. Also, her willingness to stop asking me, "Are you done writing that book?"

Annie Hoghaug and Ivy Durand, former-wife and stepdaughter-forever, who have remained close friends even though Annie and I are no longer married. Their friendship means a great deal to me; I could write with a damaged heart but probably not if it was broken. Thanks girls.

Leslie Smith-Newbury helped a great deal with the rewriting process. For two years, she found time in her extremely busy day to listen to, and even read out loud, all the stories again and again while we sipped coffee in the morning. She loved the rewriting process. Leslie also made my time living alone in the desert not lonely.

Olwen Garcia, who after our first meeting, opened her home and invited me to become her first housemate. She was a tremendous help during what could have been a much more difficult transition from married to divorced. Olwen is a voracious reader. She reviewed many early drafts and was always encouraging and honest. After several years of sharing her home, Olwen is now a very dear friend.

Two wonderful couples shared their homes with me for months while I wrote; thanks to Lee and Jules Miller, and Rich and Marie Warren.

Cindy Rogers, "Sweets," who arrived at miles twenty-four, twenty-five and twenty-six in the marathon of writing this book—the last and *the hardest*. Among her many talents she's a graphic designer and computer whiz. She used her computer skills to convert my Word documents into the publishing software necessary to print this book. Cindy scanned all of the photos and entered them into *Bat Tales*. She and I co-designed both the book and cover. Cindy braved the technical and confusing path of self-publishing with her book *Collection from an Aspen Chef*. When it was time for my journey down the same path, a couple of months later, she took me by the hand and guided me through the daunting process. She also helped me stop the endless flip flopping of words. Again and again, she answered my question, "Does this sound better, or this?" Lastly, Cindy reviewed the final draft of every story and smoothed out several places. Thanks for everything, Sweet Cindy.

Huge thanks to Pat Conway, my editor extraordinaire, co-facilitator of the Glenwood Springs Writers' Workshop (GSWW), retired library manager, poet, and devoted wife to Alan. When our writing group's other facilitator, Karen Chamberlain, passed away Pat was determined to keep the GSWW together, despite a grueling work schedule and a tough two-hour-plus commute. Amongst the hectic pace of her life, Pat somehow found time to edit *Bat Tales* and proofread the final draft. Every editing session that we had was seriously task-driven, yet painless, and oh my, did we laugh hard and have fun. Our friendship has only grown stronger during the process. Pat was *always* a believer in my work. I would also like to thank Pat's beloved husband, Alan, who radiates with angelic energy. Pat, thanks again for all of your help and faith.

Lastly, thank you, the reader. I have often said, "Everyone has a book inside them." This means each of us have experiences, interesting and exciting, difficult and heart-breaking, humorous and life affirming. Everyone's life has significance; we all have stories to share. When people found out I was writing a book many of them said, "I would love to write a book." I feel fortunate that I could find the time to write, and I'm very grateful to you—the reader—for finding the time to read my work. Thank you.

CPSIA information can be obtained
at www.ICGtesting.com
Printed in the USA
LVHW08s0752170718
584009LV00001B/3/P